OTHER BOOKS BY JOHN WESLEY ADAMS

Tenacious Love (Trinity House Press)

Wholeness Is Possible: A Paralytic Speaks Out (Trinity House Press)

Revival: It's Present Relevance & Coming Role at the End of the Age, by John Wesley Adams & Rhonda Hughey (Fusion Ministries)

The Fire Bible, by Donald C. Stamps and John Wesley Adams (Hendrickson Publishers)

"Ephesians" and "Hebrews", by John Wesley Adams. *Life in the Spirit New Testament Commentary,* editors, French L. Arrington and Roger Stronstad (Zondervan; out of print; see Amazon.com)

GOD, FIRE & REVIVAL

Supernatural Scenes & Enduring Principles

The Hebrides Revival

JOHN WESLEY ADAMS
OWEN MURPHY

Cover Design: Joshua Fenimore
Layout Artist: Les Barker
Printed in the United States of America
Library of Congress Control Number: 2016933229

Adams, John Wesley
God, Fire and Revival
ISBN 978-1-937725-37-2

Unless otherwise identified, Scripture quotations are from the New International Version of the Bible.

The Holy Bible, New International Version, Copyright © 1973, 1978, 1984 by International Bible Society. All rights reserved.

Scripture quotations marked NKJV are from the New King James Version.

The Holy Bible, New King James Version © 1979, 1980, 1982 by Thomas Nelson, Inc. All rights reserved.

TRINITY HOUSE PRESS

Trinity House Press
Kansas City, Missouri
Printed in the U.S.A.

Dedication

Dedicated to all Jesus' disciples worldwide
who are praying for a 21st century
transforming revival and spiritual awakening
that resounds to the praise of God's glory.

Contents

Prologue

This new book is a careful rewrite and significant expansion of my previous work, *The Fire Of God's Presence*. The previous book was first published in 2004 and revised in 2013. As in the previous volume, the content of this current book is the historic Hebrides revival during the mid-20th century. Supernatural scenes from that revival are vividly described here. The prayer preparation that preceded the revival and the travailing intercession that birthed it are both highlighted. Finally, enduring revival principles from that revival are featured.

Since publishing the 2004 edition, a significant primary source on the Hebrides revival has been published.[1] Aspects of its historical details are utilized here in *God, Fire And Revival*.[2]

The epicenter of the Hebrides revival was the isle of Lewis. Lewis had a rich revival history going back to the 1820's. Some intercessors in the 1949 revival had experienced a revival on the island in 1939, interrupted by World War II. Thus the isle of Lewis had "tasted" both intercession for revival and revival itself just one decade before.

As John the Baptist prepared the way for Jesus' ministry, as Savonarola prepared the way for Martin Luther, as the Moravians' "fire" helped ignite John Wesley in his revival ministry, so in revival history one revival often prepares the way for the next.

Before the Hebrides revival began in 1949, a few Hebridean people with the living memory of the 1939 revival began to pray. They had tasted the essence and power of revival a mere ten years earlier. In 1949 they saw the desperate need for it again in the church and in their community. Consequently, they began crying out to God with intense spiritual hunger for another visitation. The 1939 revival was in effect dormant seed about to sprout for the harvest of a new revival.

The 1949-53 revival was in the Hebrides' native Gaelic language. Providentially, Duncan Campbell, the main preacher God used during this visitation, could speak Gaelic[3] as well as his Scottish-English. Singing, praying, and preaching during the revival were all in Gaelic, their "heart language".[4]

My prayer is that this book will inflame your heart with fresh fire from the altar of heaven! My prayer is also that God would impart a burden for revival intercession that burns like fire in your bones and cannot be extinguished!

NOTES

[1] *Sounds from Heaven,* by Colin and Mary Peckam, is an historical documentation of the Hebrides revival by two people who were directly and indirectly close to it.

[2] *Sounds from Heaven* includes never before published material from the main preacher God used during this visitation, namely Duncan Campbell. His journal was written during those revival years. Colin and Mary Peckam, who co-authored the new book, were husband and wife, residing at Faith Mission Bible College at Edinburgh, Scotland. This is the same Bible College where Duncan Campbell was based during and after the Lewis revival. Mary experienced the Hebrides revival first-hand as a teenager. In addition to Mary's own remembrances, the book includes first-hand testimonies by other eyewitnesses from the 1949-53 revival.

[3] Gaelic is an entirely separate language.

[4] As the Hebrides is adjoined to Scotland but has its own native language Gaelic, so Wales is adjoined to England but has their own native tongue, Cymru, separate from English. Likewise, the 1904 Welsh Revival was in their native tongue or heart language, rather than English.

THE BIBLE FOR REVIVAL

LORD, I have heard of your fame;
    I stand in awe of your deeds, LORD.
        Repeat them in our day,
            in our time make them known;
                in wrath remember mercy (HABAKKUK. 3:2, NIV)

Restore us, O God;
    make your face shine on us,
    that we may be saved (PSALM 80:3 NIV).

        Restore us, O God of hosts;
            let your face shine,
            that we may be saved! (PSALM 80:7 ESV).

            Restore us, O Lord God of hosts!
                Let your face shine [REVIVAL],
                that we may be saved! (PSALM 80:7 ESV).

You will go out in joy
    and be led forth in peace;
the mountains and hills
    will burst into song before you...

Instead of the thornbush will grow the juniper,
    and instead of briers the myrtle will grow [TRANSFORMATION].

This will be for the Lord's renown,
    for an everlasting sign,
        that will endure forever (ISAIAH 55:12-13 NIV).

21ST CENTURY PRAYER FOR REVIVAL

Thank You Almighty God,

Father of our Lord Jesus Christ,

For Your fiery presence in Revival!

You alone are holy,

Only You are worthy,

God let Your Revival Fire fall!

While You pour out Your Spirit in Africa,

While You pour out Your Spirit in Asia,

While You pour out Your Spirit in Latin America,

I beseech You, pour out Your Spirit in Israel and the Middle East.

I implore You, do the same in Western nations who have rejected

You.

Jesus, never has the earth needed You more than now!

Come Holy Spirit!

Come like wind!

Come like rain!

Come like fire!

Come like oil!

Let Revival Fire come now from Your throne!

Ignite Revival Fires in our cities once again!

The Hebrides

Atlantic Ocean

Great Bernera
Lewis
Stornoway
Mealasta I.
Scarp
Seaforth I.
The Minch
Soay Mor
Taransay
Ensay
Shillay
Harris
Scalpay
Shiant Islands
St Kilda
Pabbay
Scotasay
Killegray
Boreray
Valiay
Berneray
Trodday
North Uist
Hermetray
Ascrib Is.
(South) Rona
Kirkibost I.
The Little Minch
Monach Islands
Baleshare
Ronay
Benbecula
Grimsay
Wiay
Skye
Raasay
Crowlin Is.
South Uist
Wiay
Longay
Scalpay
Pabay
Sea
Soay
Fuday
Eriskay
Canna
of the
Sanday
Rum
Mallaig
Barra
Vatersay
Eigg
Sandray
Hebrides
Mingulay
Rosinish
Muck
Berneray
Coll
Lismore
Gometra
Ulva
Eorsa
Treshnish Isles
Tiree
Staffa
Mull
Oban
Inch Kenneth
Kerrera
Iona
Seil
Erraid
Luing
Shuna
Lunga
Scarba
Colonsay
Oronsay
Jura
Danna I.
Islay
Gigha

The
Hebrides

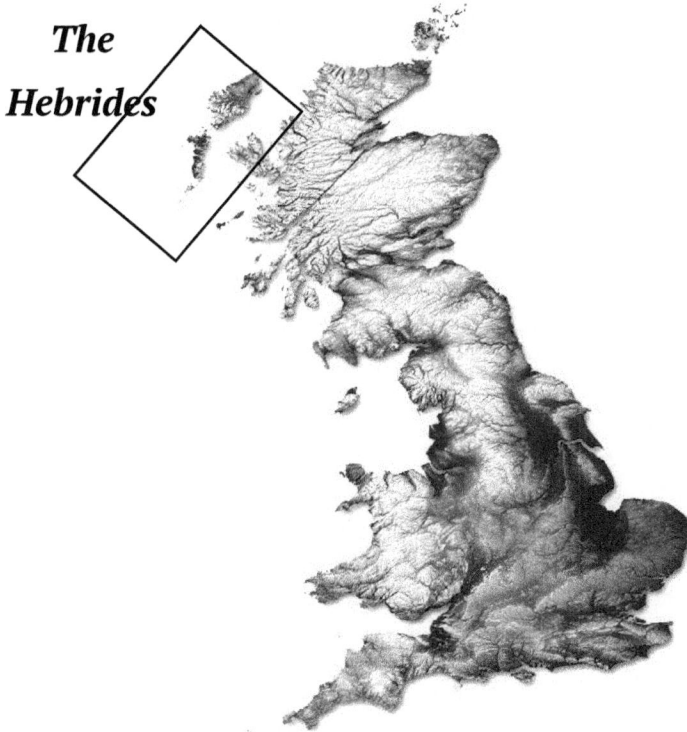

The United Kingdom

The Hebrides is a group of islands extending in an arc off the Atlantic west coast of Scotland. The islands are subdivided into two groups - the Inner Hebrides to the east and the Outer Hebrides to the west. These are separated from each other by two channels called the Minch and Little Minch[5]

[5] Hebrides" article in Encyclopedia Britannica, electronic edition, copyright 1994 - 2002.THE BIBLE FOR REVIVAL

Foreword

In the summer of 2000, a few months after the world's millennial celebrations had died down, I stood on the bridge of a Scottish ferry as it crossed a rough body of water known as The Minch. Despite a thick fog and persistent rain my spirits were high. I was, after all, on the verge of fulfilling a longstanding desire to visit the site of the famed Hebrides revival, a revival that some have called the last undisputed example of transformation in the Western world.

My sense of anticipation only heightened as I disembarked on the island of Lewis in the northernmost landmass in a chain of windswept islands known as the Outer Hebrides. Lying off the northwest coast of Scotland, these ancient rocks have seen revivals roll in with a force and regularity reminiscent of the stormy north Atlantic.

In the days that followed my arrival on Lewis, I had the extraordinary fortune to spend time with several eyewitnesses to the revival fire that is the theme of this book. Though most had slowed in body, their memories of those glorious days were as fresh and vibrant as ever. And they weren't satisfied with mere memories. "Once you've experienced revival," one misty-eyed woman explained, "you always want to see it again."

The book you now hold in your hands offers a wonderful overview of the Hebrides revival. Much of the narrative is drawn from direct witness accounts assembled by evangelist Owen Murphy in the mid-20th century. Originally published as part of a stirring booklet entitled *When God Stepped Down From Heaven*, it has been lovingly incorporated into this larger work by author Wes Adams.

Adams was a young student when Murphy brought his stirring message to Oklahoma City several decades ago. Smitten by the latter's reports of a supernatural God at work, he cast himself into a lifelong study of the principles of revival. As his knowledge grew, Wes became another valuable link in the chain of witnesses to God's glorious works and ways.

While we might be satisfied with a vivid tour of one of the last genuine revivals to grace the Western world, *God, Fire And Revival* offers something even more valuable—an examination of how and why it happened. Instead of presenting us with an elegant photo album, Adams has given us a camera with which to make our own pictures. His is a resource for activists, not spectators. If you were expecting an evening of spiritual PBS, be forewarned!

Those who elect to read on will be reminded that revival is about nothing less than an otherworldly Presence invading, and then rearranging, our temporal and fallen realm. The proposition is intoxicating, but it should come as no surprise that there are principles and preconditions to be considered. And it is here that we encounter Wes Adams at his finest, patiently explaining the ways of God in revival and then exhorting us to awaken from our slumber and embrace the fullness of our destiny.

If you are tired of spiritual games and religious inertia, if you are looking for authentic revival from heaven that results in community transformation, this is your ticket. The passionate exhortations in this book are very much in the spirit of what occurred in the Hebridean revival. And they are delivered by a man who has earned the right to share them.

George Otis, Jr.

Lynnwood, Washington

His word is in my heart like a fire,
a fire shut up in my bones.
— Jeremiah 20:9 NIV

1

A Fire Was Lit

The revival in the Hebrides, and the spiritual longings and intense intercession preceding this revival, were first introduced to me as a 20-year-old university student. An international evangelist named Owen Murphy was traveling at that time across the USA preaching and lighting revival-fire intercession in various cities.

On a cold February night, Murphy spoke in Oklahoma City. I was there and heard his fiery message. As he spoke about the Hebrides revival, he was ablaze with fresh fire from God's altar. It was contagious! This book, like the messenger that night, is a true fire-starter!

A Burning and Shining Lamp

The mid-20th century revival that spread like fire across the Hebridean islands had greatly impacted Murphy's life through Duncan Campbell (1952). The fire of the revival's reality still burned brightly in Murphy's spirit a decade later. That cold night in

Oklahoma City, like John the Baptist, Murphy was a burning and shining lamp.[1]

I listened carefully to Murphy's vivid descriptions of revival scenes in the Hebrides. As he spoke with passion, my heart began to burn like fire within me. Like the hearts of the two Emmaus-road disciples when Jesus, fresh from the gates of death, spoke to them on the day of his resurrection,[2] my heart burned!

In Oklahoma City, Owen Murphy spoke passionately about the power of prayer and exhorted the church to awaken from her spiritual slumber. Something in me came awake and alive that night! He humbly but boldly challenged us believers to humble ourselves in 2 Chronicles 7:14 fashion. He exhorted us to earnestly pray and seek God's face for revival and to repent of our own self-centered ways. As I listened to the strength of his plea, an impartation of intercessory fire for revival came upon me. My experience was somewhat similar to the experience of the prophet Jeremiah who said: *"His word is in my heart like a fire, a fire shut up in my bones. I am weary of holding it in, indeed, I cannot."*[3]

Only in retrospect, however, could I articulate clearly and understand fully that this vision-and-fire impartation had occurred. Mr. Murphy did not lay hands on any of us that night. But the fire in his heart ignited a fire in my heart! Based on the spiritual authority that he carried, he imparted vision, faith, intercession and passion for the fire of God's presence! This was similar to what was openly manifested in the Hebrides revival.

Today, after more than 50 years of revival intercession, and after more than a 1,000 hours of reading and teaching about revival, that fire still burns within me, "shut up in my bones." Such is the power of Spirit-inspired vision and the impartation of a burning heart! Such is the power of God's deposit of revival-fire in the human heart!

Healing

Toward the close of his message, Owen Murphy gave his testimony. He had been paralyzed as an adult by polio from the waist down. Five medical doctors in London (specialists) had told him that he would never walk again. Yet there he stood, that cold February night in Oklahoma City, on his feet preaching before my eyes! He was, by the power of God, completely healed and made whole. My spirit was greatly moved! And agitated!

I listened that night sitting in a wheelchair, being a quadriplegic. My spinal cord had suffered an injury from a broken neck in a car accident three and a-half years before, leaving me paralyzed from my chest down. God had given me already a personal promise of healing by the Holy Spirit and spoken to me through the Holy Scriptures about Jesus' miraculous healing ministry. I carried the hope of Jesus healing me. Why have I not yet been healed also? That night, however, my hope went to a whole new depth. For the first time in my life, I was looking at a former paralytic who was physically restored. Here was a walking miracle! Here was convincing proof that with Jesus such a miracle is indeed possible today.[4]

After hearing and pondering Owen Murphy's testimony, I learned something new! Though I could not articulate it at the time, I came to understand that God's timing for my healing related to an appointed time. I came to understand that my physical restoration was connected to the church's spiritual restoration. The time was coming when Jesus' physical healing ministry would be restored to the church as in the Book of Acts. As in Acts, this would coincide with an outpouring of the Holy Spirit's presence and power with heaven's fire.

Such an understanding can contain an element of arrogance. 1 Peter 5 states. *"God opposes the proud but shows favor to the humble."* The revelation in the previous paragraph requires patience and being clothed with humility. *"Humble yourselves, therefore, under God's mighty hand, that he may lift you up in due time. Cast all your anxiety on him because he cares for you"* (5:5-7).

A Kingdom Gem

The heart of Owen Murphy's fiery message in Oklahoma City is contained in this book. Although the February night was cold, his message was hot and passionate, truth on fire. His account of the Hebrides revival has imparted passion and heart-hunger for the fire of God's presence in multiplied thousands of people. Some churches have literally experienced a measure of revival intercession and fire when reading this account.

Nearly 3,000 books in my library have helped shape my thinking and spiritual life. Not one of these books has profoundly impacted my life more than Murphy's little booklet. Although the booklet was not copyrighted and has long since ceased being distributed, it was spiritual dynamite. A kingdom gem!

For this reason, I am incorporating Murphy's booklet in this larger book. Because Murphy was both a direct bridge back to Duncan Campbell and eyewitness testimonies about the Hebrides revival, his material is historically significant and valuable. He also powerfully captures and conveys the spiritual atmosphere and revival fervency that came when the events first occurred.

I have done careful research to identify and document Murphy's quotations and sources of information where possible. With documentation, I have also added historical facts from Duncan Campbell, and from Colin and Mary Peckham's primary resource—*Sounds from Heaven* (2004).

That being said, much of this book is a *carefully edited,* 21st century update of Murphy's original booklet. I am solely responsible for chapters 1, 2, 12 & 13. I am also responsible for portions of 3 & 4, and for carefully added [mostly historical] details throughout the book.

Covenant Prayer

This book's testimony about the power of covenant prayer (Chapter 10) is truly a challenge for believers in the Western world. This message needs to be balanced by the perspective of delayed answers to prayer that derive from human contingencies or God's sovereign timing. Nevertheless, the testimony rings true to Scripture. I commend and entrust Murphy's healing testimony to you and his miracle as an authentic sign and wonder.

NOTES

[1] John 5:35.

[2] Luke 24.

[3] Jeremiah 20:9-10.

[4] Hebrews 13:8.

Oh, that you would rend the heavens and come down, that the mountains would tremble before you! As when fire sets twigs ablaze and causes water to boil, come down to make Your name known...and cause the nations to quake before you. For when you did awesome things that we did not expect, you came down...[To act] on behalf of those who wait for [you].

—Isaiah 64:1-4

2

God's Fire Realm

The prophet Isaiah cried out for God to rend the heavens and come down like fire to make His name known. There are extraordinary times in history when God, in response to the cries and groans of His people, acts on their behalf. In great revivals He does so by opening the heavens and blanketing a community or a region with revival fire and an awesome manifestation of His fiery presence.

One such moment came in the Hebrides islands (1949-53). There God acted on behalf of some humble believers who were waiting before Him in heart-searching intercession.

How Do We Beckon Revival Fire?

Leonard Ravenhill, a personal friend of A. W. Tozer and a passionate man of prayer, greatly interceded for revival. He once had a pastor say to him: "We wish revival would come to us as it came to the Hebrides." Ravenhill replied: "But fellow servant, revival did not come to the Hebrides by wishing. The heavens were opened and the mighty power of the Lord shook those islands because 'frail children of dust ... sanctified a fast and called a solemn assembly,' and waited tear-stained, tired, and travailing before the throne of God."[1]

This book describes vivid scenes of desperate intercession and the fire of God's awesome and holy presence that is manifest when He rends the heavens and comes down in authentic revival fire and spiritual awakening.

God's Presence Is Like Fire

Why is God's presence like fire? Because God is like fire! Of the more than 500 Bible references to fire, 90 of them are associated directly with God & His Presence. Fire is an essential characteristic of God.

"The Lord your God is a consuming fire, a jealous God."[2] The same description of God is repeated under the new covenant. In the New Testament it is writen: *"Let us offer to God acceptable worship, with reverence and awe, for our God is a consuming fire."*[3]

When Moses was on the mountain with God in the wilderness, the glory of Yahweh, to the Israelites, looked like a consuming fire on top of the mountain (Exodus 24:17). The fire of God's holiness reveals all that is unholy and judges all that is evil. Psalm 97:3 declares, "Fire goes before Him and consumes his foes on every side." 2 Thessalonians 1:7 says that the Lord

Jesus will be revealed from heaven "in blazing fire with his powerful angels."

Elijah, the prophet of God to apostate Israel, confronted Israel's King Ahab and his Baal worshipping wife Jezebel. God instructed Elijah to challenge Jezebel's false Baal prophets to a contest on Mount Carmel. The contest was at the end of a three and a half year drought when there was no rain—zero! God intended the event to settle for Israel who was the real and true God and therefore who controlled the rain.

Elijah instructed the Baal prophets to build an altar to their false god and placed an animal sacrifice on it. The Israelites were to stand-by as witnesses. Elijah said to the Israelites: *"How long will you falter between two opinions? If the Lord is God, follow Him; but if Baal, follow him."* Then Elijah challenged the 450 Baal prophets to cut in pieces their bull sacrifice *"and lay it on the wood, but put no fire under it; and I will prepare the other bull, and lay it on the wood, but put no fire under it. Then you call on the name of your gods, and I will call on the name of the Lord; and the God who answers by fire, He is God."*[4]

Jezebel's false prophets could not get an answer by fire, though they called out from morning to evening. At the time of the evening sacrifice, Elijah stepped forward. He had men pour four barrels of water from the sea over the altar and his sacrifice, soaking the wood and sacrifice, and running down till the trench around the altar was filled with water. Then Elijah prayed a short prayer of 41 Hebrew words! At the end of his prayer, *"the fire of the Lord fell and consumed the burnt sacrifice, and the wood and the stones and the dust, and it licked up the water that was in the trench. Now when all the people saw it, they fell on their faces; and they said, 'The Lord, He is God! The Lord, He is God!'"*[5]

Fire At the Throne

What is God like? God is like fire! A God of heavenly and eternal fire!

When Moses encountered God's holy presence at the burning bush, it was as fire. Ezekiel had an awesome vision of God's presence and glory coming in a windstorm as fire.[6]

Ezekiel's account is awe inspiring and mind-baffling! In the midst of a stunning configuration of supernatural fire, a sapphire throne and a figure similar to that of a man appeared. From the *"waist up he looked like glowing metal, as if full of fire, ...from there down he looked like fire; and brilliant light surrounded him."*[7] Ezekiel adds: *"This was the appearance of the likeness of the glory of the* LORD.*"*[8] Ezekiel's response to this revelation was to fall forward, face down and awestruck!

Even the four living creatures accompanying God's mobile throne had the appearance of fire. *"Their appearance was like burning coals of fire, like the appearance of torches moving to and fro among the living creatures. And the fire was bright, and out of the fire went forth lightning. And the living creatures darted to and fro, like the appearance of a flash of lightning.*"[9]

Equally stunning is Daniel's vision of God as the Ancient of Days seated on His throne ablaze with fire. Daniel records that *a river of fire was flowing, coming out from before him [God].*[10]

Jesus revealed himself to the godly apostle John in John's old age. John beheld Jesus on that occasion as the Son of Man whose *eyes were like a flame of fire, his feet were like burnished bronze, refined in a furnace, and his voice was like the roar of many waters. In his right hand he held seven stars, from his mouth came a sharp two-edged sword, and his face was like the sun shining in full strength.*[11] What was John's response? In John's own words, when *I saw him, I fell at his feet as though dead.*[12]

Who can stand in the presence of God? Isaiah presented the question long ago, *Who of us can dwell with the consuming fire? Who of us can dwell with everlasting burning?*[13]

In Revelation 4, John saw flashes of fire like lightning going forth from God's fiery throne. Before the throne on the sea of glass, like crystal, were burning seven "torches of fire", which are the seven spirits of God (4:2, 5). In the heavenly throne room, God is not like an iceberg but like a majestic flame of fire. His glory and holiness are brighter than the sun's rays in all its strength. From His sapphire throne God carries out His great purposes with burning desire and His mighty deeds with fire off the altar of intercession.

God's universe is full of fire. The sun in our solar system as well as every star in every constellation shines by the fire that God created. At the center of planet earth is a molten core of fire. Every volcano is a reminder that the Creator is a God of fire.

God Is the Spirit of Burning

When it was time for God to deliver His people from the slavery of Egypt, He shifted them into position so He could fulfill His promises that He had made many years before to Abraham about a promised land. When doing so, God manifest His presence amongst His people in a *pillar of fire* by night and a cloud by day.

God had manifested himself to Moses at a **burning bush** that was not consumed. From the midst of its flames, God spoke profound words of instruction to Moses and revealed His name as the eternal "I AM". Now he manifests his presence to Israel as a pillar of fire that burned continually through the darkness of the night, night after night. Yahweh is a God of fire. His Spirit is a Spirit of burning.

In Isaiah the Messiah, is described as the Branch of the Lord that will appear in Israel:

In that day the Branch of the Lord shall be beautiful and glorious. And the fruit of the earth shall be excellent and appealing for those of Israel who have escaped. And it shall come to pass that he who is left in Zion and remains in Jerusalem will be called holy—everyone who is recorded among the living in Jerusalem. When the Lord has washed away the filth of the daughters of Zion, and purged the blood of Jerusalem from her midst, by the spirit of judgment and by the **spirit of burning***, then the Lord will create above every dwelling place of Mount Zion, and above her assemblies, a cloud and smoke by day and . . .* ***a flaming fire by night.***[14]

In this passage Isaiah is not referring to Israel's past, but to Israel's future. As during the great Exodus event [PAST], so it will be in the day when the Messiah reigns in Jerusalem [FUTURE]. God's presence will again be manifested as a cloud by day and a flaming fire by night.

When it was time for God to give birth to His church, God again marked that great moment in redemptive history with fire. As the Spirit of fire, the Holy Spirit, descended on 120 praying believers on the Day of Pentecost, the occasion was marked by ***"what seemed to be tongues of fire*** *that separated and came to rest on each of them."*[15] The Spirit of God is a Spirit of fire. When God began His church, there was fire. Whenever God visits His church in revival, there is fire. Revival always comes with Holy Spirit fire.

Hebrews says God makes His angels ministering spirits and **His ministers flames of fire.**[16] Elijah called fire down from heaven, and when he died he went to heaven in chariots of fire. Elijah was a fire man. Jesus said concerning *John the Baptist, "He was a burning and shining lamp, and you were willing to rejoice for a while in his light."*[17] The Baptist was a fire man! *John Wesley* once prayed, "God set me on fire and people will come to see me burn." John Wesley was a fire man! A century later, *William Booth* and his wife Catherine raised up the "salvation army" and they were burning and shining lamps in the darkness of East London's slums. Their slogan was "Blood and Fire." The Booths' army burned with heaven's fire. This is the kind of God we serve, a God who answers by fire!

Jon Thurlow's song—STORM ALL AROUND YOU —describes the heavenly throne room scene:

> *I see seven lamps of fire burning,*
> *And I see a sea of glass mingled with fire burning,*
> *I see the Son of Man with eyes of fire burning,*
> *Burning, burning, burning.*

God's heart yearns and desires a people who know the reality of His fiery love and who burn with love for Him. Leonard Ravenhill once said, "Snowmen in the pulpits with icicles hanging all around" will melt when the fire of God's presence appears.

Fire of God's Holiness

The church in the 21st century desperately needs an encounter with the fire of God's glory and holiness. Encountering the fire of God's presence will instantly expose our pride, our impure motives, our hidden sin and our shallow relationship with Him. His fire will inescapably create a holy and reverential fear of God and His judgments. His fire will immediately bring sinners and saints alike into a sober awareness of His holiness and the awfulness of our sin. His fire will inspire sincere humility, deep biblical repentance and true faith in Jesus Christ alone for salvation.

In the Hebrides, all of the above happened as God's fiery presence was manifested on a local, community and a regional scale.

Throughout Scripture "fire" is a symbol of **God's presence,**[18] **God's power,**[19] and **God's purity.**[20] It is not without significance that the words *purify* and *purge* come from the Greek word for fire. "What a call this is to Christian people to purify themselves by the fire of the Word of God[21] and the fire of the Spirit of God[22] to be the instruments of a mighty conflagration that burns the barriers to revival and brings the blessing of revival!"[23]

Dr. W. Graham Scroggie once said, "There never has been a spiritual revival which did not begin with an acute sense of sin. We are never prepared for a spiritual advance until we see the necessity of getting rid of that which has been hindering it, and that, in the sight of God, is sin."[24]

God's promise is clear: "If My people who are called by My name will humble themselves, and pray and seek My face, and turn from their wicked ways, then I will hear from heaven, and will forgive their sin and heal their land."[25]

Fire of God's Love

The fire of God's love burns most brightly and is seen most widely during revival. Psalm 89:1 says, "*I will sing of the Lords great love for ever.*" God's loves is so vast that He loved the whole world in the giving of His Son.[26] The third verse of the hymn, "The Love of God", expresses the vastness of God's love with these descriptive words:

> *Could we with ink the ocean fill,*
> *And were the skies of parchment made,*
> *Were every stalk on earth a quill,*
> *And every man a scribe by trade,*
> *To write the love of God above,*
> *Would drain the ocean dry.*
> *Nor could the scroll contain the whole,*
> *Though stretched from sky to sky.*[27]

In times of great revival, sinners and saints all encounter the intensity of God's love as a hot flame. Converts with great joy sing about God's love, testify about God's love, tell other people about God's love as they glow with love's flame.

God is not a stone-cold emotionless deity! God is love, and He burns with holy desire and affection for those for whom Jesus died. God's love is not cold theology! He is love that burns like a flame for those whom He has created and seeks to redeem. God, who has everything and needs nothing, still has burning desire because He is love. God's fiery love burns, not out of need, but from the fountainhead of overflowing desire for those whom He created in His image. The measure of the Father's affection for His Son, Jesus, is the measure of His affection for all His sons and daughters. Only God's love can fully satisfy our heart's desire for love and intimacy. During revival, the fire of God's love is living revelation, a spiritual knowing that burns like spiritual passion.

You were created for love. True love originates with God. You have the capacity to love because God is love. You cannot be whole until you encounter God's love for you and are able to respond to Him wholeheartedly with love.

God's love is described as *the very flame of the LORD* (Song of Songs 8:6 ESV). Love's flame will burn on and on forever because it is the LORD's flame. He burns with love! Revelation and experience of God's fiery love, and growing in the knowledge of His love "more and more"[28] is the key for entering into God's heart and enjoying Him forever.

Fire of God's Power

In Revelation 4, John saw flashes of fire *like lightning* going forth from God's throne. Lightning here is not the phenomenon that meteorologist speak of in their weather forecasts. This lightning is strictly the phenomena of God. It is similar to what Habakkuk the prophet saw. God's power was flashing like rays of light, going forth from His hands:

> *His splendor was like the sunrise;*
> *rays flashed from **his hand**,*
> *where his power was hidden.*[29]

Habakkuk 3:2-4 describes revival as the visitation of God to His people in glory and power. Jonathan Edwards described revival as "the Day of God's Power."[30]

God's "hand" that Habakkuk saw in heaven has its counterpart here on earth in the anointed hands of His people releasing His power. God's hand thus refers to the hand of anointed, sanctified vessels through whom God releases His power for physical healing and miracles.

Peter and other believers raised their voices together and petitioned God: "stretch forth your **hand** to heal and perform signs and wonders through the name of your holy servant Jesus."[31] God answered this prayer by releasing a healing revival of power through the hands of Peter and others a short time later. That release of healing power is described in Acts 5:12 as follows:

*Through **the hands** of the apostles many signs and wonders were done among the people. And believers were increasingly added to the Lord, multitudes of both men and women, so that they brought the sick out into the streets and laid them on beds and couches, that at least the shadow of Peter passing by might fall on some of them. Also a multitude gathered from the surrounding cities to Jerusalem, bringing sick people and those who were tormented by unclean spirits, and **they were all healed**.* [32]

In 1947-48, at the very time Israel was becoming a nation again, a huge healing revival burst forth suddenly in the United States and Canada like a mighty ocean wave.[33] Many thousands of people with incurable diseases and infirmities were miraculously healed.[34]

A healing revival is very much on God's heart and also on His calendar for the last days. Rays of light (like lightning bolts of power) hidden in the palm of the hand will go forth to heal the sick, infirmed and demonized in nation after nation.

There were three major features in Jesus' earthly ministry: preaching, teaching and healing.[35] These same three features of preaching, teaching and healing will characterize the coming great revival. The lightning bolts of God will strike with convincing power and proof that *"Jesus Christ is the same yesterday and today and forever."*[36]

Revival Realm Is the Fire Realm

Fire is light, bright, hot, burns, full of energy, roars, glows, illuminates, spreads, purges, cleanses, purifies, refines, tests and consumes. The fire of God has all these characteristics. So does revival!

Preceding this volume, two notable revival books have FIRE in their title:

1) *Revival Fire* by Wesley Duewel, and 2) *Firefall: How God Has Shaped History Through Revivals* by Malcolm McDow and A. L. Reid. Why do these two revival books have "Fire" in their title? The answer is simple: FIRE is a foremost *spiritual and supernatural* component of authentic revival. This is because a primary element of God's presence and holiness is symbolized by fire.

As we have seen in this chapter, the Bible is full of references about the fiery make-up of God's very existence. Not surprising, therefore, when God supernaturally manifests His presence on the earth in revival by visiting His people in great salvation, there is always the element of fire. Thus the title of this book: *God, Fire & Revival.*

Jesus said, *I have come **to cast fire on the earth** and how I wish it were already kindled.*[37] "Revival fire" is certainly one of those fires that Jesus came to cast on the earth. And He wished it were already kindled when He spoke His words!

William Booth, founder of the Salvation Army and himself a flaming evangelist, captured the relevance and supremacy of the fire of God when he wrote in 1894 the hymn, "*SEND THE FIRE.*" Consider the hot, burning flame of truth in the following passionate words:

Thou Christ of burning, cleansing flame,
Send the fire, send the fire, send the fire!
Thy blood-bought gift today we claim,
Send the fire, send the fire, send the fire!
Look down and see this waiting host,
Give us the promised Holy Ghost;
We want another Pentecost,
Send the fire, send the fire, send the fire!

God of Elijah, hear our cry:
Send the fire, send the fire, send the fire!
To make us fit to live or die,
Send the fire, send the fire, send the fire!
To burn up every trace of sin,
To bring the light and glory in,
The revolution now begin,
Send the fire, send the fire, send the fire!

'Tis fire we want, for fire we plead,
Send the fire, send the fire, send the fire!
The fire will meet our every need,
Send the fire, send the fire, send the fire!
For strength to ever do the right,
For grace to conquer in the fight,

For pow'r to walk the world in white,
Send the fire, send the fire, send the fire!

To make our weak hearts strong and brave,
Send the fire, send the fire, send the fire!
To live a dying world to save,
Send the fire, send the fire, send the fire!
Oh, see us on Thy altar lay
Our lives, our all, this very day;
To crown the off'ring now we pray,
Send the fire, send the fire, send the fire

NOTES

[1] Leonard Ravenhill, *Why Revival Tarries* (Minneapolis: Bethany Fellowship, 1959), p. 131.

[2] Deuteronomy 4:24.

[3] Hebrews 12:28-29.

[4] 1 Kings 18:23-24.

[5] 1 Kings 18:38-39.

[6] Ezekiel 1:4-28.

[7] Ezekiel 1:27.

[8] Ezekiel 1:28.

[9] Ezekiel 1:13-14.

[10] Daniel 7:9c, 10a.

[11] Revelation 1:14-16.

[12] Revelation 1:17.

[13] Isaiah 33:14.

[14] Isaiah 4:2-5.

[15] Acts 2:3, NIV.

[16] Hebrews 1:7.

[17] John 5:35.

[18] Genesis 15:17; Exodus 3:2; 13:21-22, et al.

[19] Exodus 19:18; 24:17; 1 Kings 18:24, 38.

[20] Isaiah 6:6.

[21] Jeremiah 5:14.

[22] Acts 2:3.

[23] Stephen Olford, "Foreword" in *Revival Fire* by Wesley Duewel Grand Rapids: Zondervan, 1995), pg. 10.

[24] Ibid.

[25] 2 Chron. 7:14 NKJV.

[26] John 3:16.

[27] Frederick M. Lehman, Hymn: "The Love of God."

[28] Philippians 1:9 NKJV.

[29] Habakkuk 3:4, NIV.

[30] Jonathan Edwards as quoted in J. I. Packer, *A Quest for Godliness: The Puritan Vision of the Christian Life* (Wheaton, Illinois: Crossway Books, 1990), 323.

[31] Acts 4:30.

[32] Acts 5:12, 14-16.

[33] 1947-58

[34] David Edwin Harrell, Jr. *All Things are Possible: The Healing and Charismatic Revivals in Modern America* (Bloomington, IN: Indiana University Press, 1975). This is the definitive history of the Healing Revival, 1947-1958; well written and carefully documented.

[35] Matthew 4:23-25.

[36] Hebrews 13:8.

[37] Luke 12:49, NASB.

This is revival in the Hebrides!

When men and women in the streets are afraid to speak godless words for fear that God's judgment will fall, this is revival from heaven! When awakened sinners are suddenly aware of the fire of God's presence, tremble in the streets and cry out for mercy, this is revival from heaven! When, without human advertising, the Holy Spirit sweeps across cities and towns in supernatural power and holds people in the grip of terrifying conviction, revival fire has come! When every store becomes a pulpit, every heart an altar, every home a sanctuary and every person walks carefully before God - this is God-given revival from His throne room in heaven!

3

Revival From Heaven

Restore us, O God; make your face shine on us, that we may be saved.—Psalm 80:3 NIV

Today the word "revival" has largely lost its true meaning. Since most Christians in this generation have never witnessed the mighty moving of God in nation-wide spiritual awakening, they have little concept of the magnitude of such a visitation.

Revival is often confused with evangelism. God-sent revival is not synonymous with large conferences, crusades or concerts where people come to hear outstanding preachers or musicians. Neither is revival the result of an effective advertising blitz that draws large crowds to special campaigns and regional meetings. In a God-sent revival, leaders need not spend money on advertising. People will come whenever and wherever there is the fire of God's presence. Such is the nature and characteristic of revival from heaven!

Historic, transforming revival comes with widespread acute awareness of God that impacts an entire community. Transformation includes not just the church, but also schools, the marketplace, public transportation, businesses, entertainment, local government, etc. Taverns, bars, discos and nightclubs, for lack of customers, are often closed down. Lord, do it again! Immorality is no longer a common and acceptable lifestyle. Lord, do it again! These transforming results occur because people repent of their sin and find salvation, love, joy and peace alone in Jesus Christ! This is revival from heaven!

There is a vast difference between modern evangelistic campaigns and revival from heaven. In evangelistic campaigns, hundreds may be brought to a saving knowledge of Jesus Christ. That is wonderful! Churches may experience God's refreshing. That too is glorious! However, as far as the community, city or region is concerned, little impact happens. Community transformation does not follow. Sin continues to abound at all levels of society and godlessness continues to advance unhindered.

However, when revival from heaven occurs, the fire of God's Spirit sweeps through society as a cleansing flame. Hearts are awakened and solemn conviction of sin touches people everywhere. The strongholds of the devil shake and crumble! Many public places of sinful pleasure close down! Why? Because so many people are turning to Jesus Christ in repentance and faith, and subsequently *forsaking* their former lifestyle of sin.

REVIVAL FROM HEAVEN | 49

American Revival of 1857-59

This notable "prayer meeting revival" began in the marketplace as the result of the obedience of one man, Jeremiah Lanphier. Mr. Lanphier distributed pamphlets inviting businessmen to join him during their lunch hour to pray for their city. Beginning in lower Manhattan, this revival ignited as men responded to pray during their lunch break. God's fire ignited revival fire and the fire spread quickly! Revival flames within six months spread from New York City across the United States to the west coast.

The revival was like a spiritual forest fire. The redemptive flames of God's Spirit spread rapidly! New England became the center of an enormous spiritual awakening that resulted in great numbers of people experiencing forgiveness of their sins and the reality of salvation through faith in Jesus Christ alone. In some towns the report was that it was "almost impossible to find anyone who had not been converted."[1]

Like a great spiritual epidemic, tremendous conviction of sin swept through the land, and thousands turned to Christ. Drunkards standing at the bars, gamblers sitting at card tables, people gathered in churches, and even passengers on ships as they approached land found themselves suddenly aware of God's presence and holiness. Overcome before Him, they repented of their sins, finding forgiveness and eternal life.

In towns and cities across America—bars, theaters and gambling establishments closed or emptied; new churches began to spring up; family altars were established or restored; and the spirit of prayer grew in intensity. Eventually anyone crossing the United States could find a "midday" prayer meeting in almost any town. When this gracious revival was at its height, as many as 50,000 people a week experienced God's saving grace in Jesus Christ.

Following in the wake of America's 1857-59 Revival came mighty preachers of God's Word such as D.L. Moody. Under his ministry multitudes experienced salvation through faith in Jesus Christ. The Student Volunteer Movement was formed, which challenged college students in the universities to surrender and volunteer their lives to serve Jesus overseas. The impact was considerable! Pioneer missionaries were raised up by God and commissioned to go with the gospel to the ends of the earth. This is the fruit of revival! Yes, Lord, do it again!

Welsh Revival of 1904

The year 1904 stands out in the history of Wales as a year that will never be forgotten. Fifty years later those who were privileged and blessed to live in those revival days still spoke of its supernatural scenes with the greatest of awe.

The Spirit of God, like a mighty fire driven by the wind, swept across the land, until mountains and valleys, cities and villages were filled with mighty manifestations of God. In this little country, churches were crowded and meetings went on day after day, night after night, week after week, month after month for two full years. Prayer, singing and testimonies would sweep over congregations in torrents as hundreds and thousands were turning to Christ—100,000 converted in the first five months alone. Never in the history of Wales had such indescribable scenes been witnessed.

G. Campbell Morgan, having just visited the Welsh revival, returned home to London where he preached on Sunday Christmas evening, 25th December 1904, in the famous Westminster Chapel. In his message on "Lessons of the Welsh Revival", Morgan declared boldly:

In...the Welsh revival there is no preaching, no [leader-led] order, no hymnbooks, no choirs, no organs, no collections, and finally, no advertising. Now, think of that for a moment, again, will you? There were the organs, but silent; the ministers [were there], but among the rest of the people, rejoicing and prophesying with the rest, only there was no preaching. Yet, the Welsh Revival is "the revival of preaching to Wales". Everybody is preaching. No order, yet it moves from day to day, week to week, county to county, with matchless precision, with the order of an attacking force. No [song} books, but ah me, I nearly wept tonight over the singing of our last hymn. . . . When these Welshmen sing, they sing the words like men who believe them. They abandon themselves to their singing. We sing as though we thought it would not be respectable to be heard by the one next to us. No choir, did I say? It was all choir.[2]

At year's end (1904), the Welsh Sunday schools, the Bible classes and the family devotionals were flourishing because of the revival and reaping their harvests. Wales was ablaze for God! 20,000 converts were recorded in five weeks and 50,000 in three months. This nation's spiritual awakening showed no sign of diminishing. It swept over hundreds of villages and cities—emptying taverns, theaters and dance halls, and filling the churches night after night with praying multitudes. Go where you will, into the bank, the store, the trains, and everywhere people are talking about God.

If you could stand above Wales, looking down on it during the revival, you would see, without any human planning, the fire of God's presence breaking out here-there-and-everywhere. It is a divine visitation in which God—let me say this reverently—in which God is saying to us: "*See what I can do without the things you are depending on. See what I can do through a praying people who are prepared to depend wholly and absolutely upon me.*"[3]

Wales was moved by the presence and the power of God, until almost every home in the nation felt its impact like a tree shaken by a mighty storm. Newspapers carried the news of the amazing scenes taking place. So great was the fear of God and conviction of sin that gripped the people that in some communities crime disappeared. Judges were presented with a blank paper, as no cases waited to be tried. And to commemorate the occasion, they were presented with white gloves.

In more than one location the post office's supply of money orders were exhausted as people, seeking to make restitution, paid their debts! Bars and theaters closed! Stores sold out of Bibles and Testaments. Members of parliament, who were busy attending revival services, postponed their political meetings. Theatrical companies coming into districts found no audiences, for "all the world was praying." Temperance workers, in three months, saw the Spirit of God accomplish more than they had accomplished in 40 years.[4]

Hebrides Revival

In the Hebrides, as in Wales, revival happened in answer to the cries of God's people. Men and women, in travail before God, fell on their knees. Revival is a visitation of the Holy Spirit pouring intense conviction of sin upon the ungodly. Whether in the church, in the marketplace, in the classroom or in a variety of other locations, multitudes were turning in tear-stained repentance to Christ. Such then is REVIVAL—the mighty, widespread saturation of God's presence and Kingdom in a region!

NOTES

[1] From a taped message by Duncan Campbell, originally delivered to the students of the Faith Mission Bible College in Edinburgh, Scotland.

[2] G. Campbell Morgan, "Lessons of the Welsh Revival," in S.B. Shaw. *The Great Revival in Wales* (Salem, OH: Allegheny Publications, 1988 reprint; originally published in 1905), pp. 74-75.

[3] S.B. Shaw. *The Great Revival in Wales* (1905). Scattered references

[4] Ibid.

4

Will It Happen Again?

Will you not revive us again, that your people may rejoice in you?—Psalm 85:6 NIV

With all the aforementioned great revivals now past history, we ask: "Can those same *events* be repeated?" "Should they be repeated?" "Will they be repeated?" "Should we even pray and expect such events to occur again?" "Will God send a similar revival from heaven in our day?"

Revival history is progressively linear, not circular.[1] God seldom does anything exactly the same way twice. Nevertheless, God can and will *revive us again*, but He will do *more* than He has done in the past. God builds on the past and *surpasses* the past. The past inspires us to pray for the next and *larger* redemptive intervention that God has planned for his people.

God emphasizes this in Isaiah 48:

I foretold the former things long ago, ...
then suddenly I acted, and they came to pass. . . .

From now on I will tell you of new things,
of hidden things unknown to you.
They are created now, and not long ago;
you have not heard of them before [i.e., in times past].[2]

God is waiting to do even greater things than He has done in the past great revivals! In every generation the revival resources of God are increasing and waiting to be released. When God finds people who will stand before Him with desperate spiritual hunger, clean hands and pure hearts, true humility, persevering intercession, and bold faith that make revival possible, He will yet again release revival fire from heaven!

In another book titled REVIVAL that I co-authored, this point is developed in greater detail. Here is further explanation of important truth about the progressive nature of great revivals:

The Bible reveals that history is moving forward in purposeful progression from a God-initiated beginning to a God-appointed end. God transcends history as the Creator, descends into history as the Redeemer, and will return as the Bridegroom to unite with His prepared Bride to rule with Him in an ever increasing and expanding Kingdom (Rev. 19:6, 9; 21:7, 9, 10).

In the progressive unfolding of redemptive history toward its end-time goal, revival history plays an important and even crucial role in the outcome! Revival is a catalyst to advance the church from its present state to the next level of restoration on the road to the fullness of God's glory in the earth.

Just as redemption is necessary because of the fall and sinfulness of humanity, so revival is necessary because of the church's tendency to spiritual decline!

Therefore God's larger revival purpose must be viewed in the context of redemption, and more specifically in the context of the progressive nature of redemption. A macro read of church history reveals a divine pattern. God has been restoring and shaping the church through the catalytic impact of historic revivals since the Protestant Reformation.[3]

For those who travel the highways of the world, there are encouraging signs that God is again "preparing the way" for a new spiritual awakening. The Hebrides islands during their three years of revival was the scene of some of the most stirring revival moments in the mid-twentieth century. This inspiring revival challenges men and women everywhere to *stand in the gap and make up the hedge[4]* for revival in this generation.

The spiritual awakening in the Hebrides (1949-53) continues to challenge and inspire intercessors and the hearts of God's people everywhere. This is not because of the magnitude of its size, but rather because of the intensity of God's pre*sence that was openly manifested there in extraordinary strength in response to their prayers.*

The physical conditions in the Hebrides were not conducive for a stirring awakening. The islands were scattered, their population were not dense, transport was difficult, and the land was rugged and the people unemotional. In spite of all this, still large numbers of people turned to Christ in life-changing conversions. The supernatural character of this revival is further evident in the fact that 75% of all those who were saved during the revival were saved outside of any church building.[5]

This should infuse each one of our nations with fresh vision and new faith that a great spiritual awakening can happen outside of our church buildings.

The news of the great Prayer Meeting Revival of America in 1857-59 swept across the ocean and brought revival to Ireland in 1859. So, in God's strategy, what God did in the Hebrides *in response to prayer* was meant to challenge the church and its intercessors in America and elsewhere to pray until the flames of revival are again kindled everywhere. Only then will God's fire sweep across this whole land in a mighty outpouring of the Holy Spirit.

God Has Visited His People

In the summer of 1952, a great crowd of people, drawn from every part of the earth to the world-famous Keswick Convention in England, had just heard the electrifying message by Duncan Campbell about that

Hebrides revival. Slowly the crowd began to file out of the big convention tent. Suddenly a woman in an awe-struck voice exclaimed: "It was just as though God had stepped out of heaven!"

Keswick ConventionTent

And so it seemed to me also [O. Murphy]! I too sat spellbound listening to the most thrilling, faith-inspired message I had ever heard. The message was destined to sweep across the face of the earth, stirring men and women to seek the face of God as never before. The news was about the gracious visitation of God's presence to the Hebrides.

Never in its many years of history had the Keswick Convention been more mightily stirred, as it listened to the report of the amazing events that had taken place just a few hundred miles away. The reports were that "hundreds had been converted; many conversions occurred without a word being spoken to them. Apart from church buildings, sinners in various places were trembling under conviction. While people gathered in churches to pray, great conviction of sin was sweeping over entire districts. Sinners were falling helpless along the roads. Multiple church meetings were lasting for hours, services were being held nightly, churches and communities were being transformed. A preacher was called at four o'clock in the morning to pray with men and women outside the police station. These people, who had been smitten with great conviction of sin, were crying for God to have mercy on them!"

Hebridean Homes along the Coastline of the Island of Lewis

The vivid descriptions of the Hebrides at the Keswick Convention reminded the people of the great Welsh Revival of 1904. Their hearts were being gripped by what they were hearing! They remembered the amazing events of those historic days in Wales when meetings were held day and night, and churches were packed to capacity as thousands turned to Christ. Because of lack of patronage, theaters and taverns were closed. Thieves and murderers surrendered to the Lord, and police courts were idle. Sins were confessed and old debts were paid. Work was forgotten for a time, and meetings frequently would last all night and days at a time.

Christmas 1904 was the first real Christmas many children in Wales, and even men and women, ever had. Instead of being spent in taverns, as before, hard-earned wages were used for groceries and toys. The poverty of former days had been replaced with joy and plenty, for Christ had been invited into thousands of homes. Virtually the whole of Wales was on its knees on Christmas Day. That revival lasted about four years and swept through England, Ireland, parts of Europe, and even crossed the oceans to Australia and America, changing the lives of multiple thousands.

Spiritual leaders and workers from various denominations who were present at that unforgettable meeting in Keswick, England were stirred, as they had never been before. They returned to their churches to call their people to prayer, convinced that another great revival and spiritual awakening was going to break forth in the world.

Rouse America To Pray

Slowly the large crowd was leaving the convention tent and filling the long narrow streets of the little market town of Keswick. As all this was unfolding, a man stood at my side and spoke to me. He was the very man [Duncan Campbell] whom God had used so remarkably in the Hebrides awakening. I can still hear his closing words of challenge:

When you return to America, rouse the people; tell them what God is doing! I believe every church can have what we are having in the Hebrides. There is no 'mystery', but there is a 'secret'. If God can find a people over there, prepared to 'pay the price' as they have over here, He will visit them in the same revival of power!

Every word that fell from his lips seemed to burn its way into my soul. I became conscious that the Spirit of God was speaking to me and giving me a new commission. As I remembered the tremendous impact of the message upon that large crowd of people that afternoon at Keswick, a great conviction gripped me. That message was surely for me, and also the message that all ministers and churches throughout the world needed to hear. Canceling my evangelistic campaigns, I returned immediately to America to stir her people to seek the face of God so that a similar spiritual awakening might happen there.

The impact in America of this dynamic message about God's visitation in the Hebrides has been amazing. Powerful prayer groups have sprung up everywhere, and church prayer meetings have been revitalized. In many churches the "all-night" prayer meeting has been restored, or introduced for the first time. The results of this resurgence of prayer is a real moving of the Spirit of God in conviction, confession of sin and reconsecration. This happened with both ministers and congregations alike. In some towns the churches interceded before God for their entire community as they held citywide all-night prayer meetings.

Devout ministers of all denominations, burdened for real revival, sought God in fasting and prayer on behalf of their churches. Many witnessed gracious manifestations of God among their congregations. At times preachers were unable to deliver their sermons. The Spirit of God quietly swept through congregations, convicting people of their sin. Oftentimes groups of people spontaneously would walk down the aisles to kneel, sobbing at the altars and confessing their sins. This without a word being preached to them!

Camp meetings, Bible colleges and conferences have been challenged and stirred, while large numbers of people have been swept to the altars, confessing their sin and embracing Jesus Christ as Savior. Churches with real hunger for revival from heaven eagerly await this message to be taken to them.

We realize the utter impossibility of personally reaching every church with this spoken message. We are also conscious of the desperate need for Christians everywhere to face up to the challenge of this tremendous message. What is the urgent message? Answer: that a real revival from heaven come to this nation! Therefore, this message is being sent forth in written form. With it goes our earnest prayer that wherever this message goes, the blessings of revival shall follow.

The content of this book is largely based on either *personal interviews* with people who were participants in the Hebrides revival or derived from *published investigative reports*. I [Owen Murphy] have made no attempt either to minimize or to exaggerate details of this gracious visitation. Realizing that when a number of reports describe the same events, some minor differences will occur. This is true even among the four Gospel accounts of Jesus' resurrection in the Bible. Unlike Scripture, however, we make no claim for perfect accuracy or inerrancy in the chronology of every event or in minor details. Nevertheless, we have been careful to be as accurate as possible.

The gracious manifestation of God's presence in the Hebrides, the intercession that preceded it and the community transformation that accompanied it are a deposit of what God longs to do with the church today on a large scale. The Hebrides revival reveals the potential power of prayer for the greatest sovereign moving of God in revival power that any generation has ever known.

We are a continuation of history. God is inviting His people in this generation to join with the history makers and shakers of past revivals to advance God's kingdom forward to its ultimate goal.

May you hear in this book a personal challenge to pray fervently for both revival and transformation in the city or region of the earth where God has placed you!

NOTES

[1] For an explanation and development of this point, see John Wesley Adams and Rhondda Hughey, Revival: Its Present Relevance and Coming Role At the End of the Age (Fusion Ministries, 2010) pp. 85-109.

[2] Isaiah 48:3, 6-7.

[3] Ibid., pg. 86.

[4] Ezekiel 22:30

[5] From a taped message by Duncan Campbell, originally delivered to the students of the Faith Mission Bible College in Edinburgh, Scotland.

Prepare the way for the Lord;
make straight in the desert a highway for
our God. . . .
And the glory of the Lord will be revealed,
and all people will see it together.
For the mouth of the Lord has spoken.
—Isaiah 40:3, 5

5

How the Hebrides Revival Began

Prayer preparation preceded the Holy Spirit descending at Pentecost.[1] It is historically true that prayer preparation always precedes revival! The Word of God, the testimony of history, and the gracious visitation of God to the Hebrides all emphasize this very truth: prayer preparation must begin with God's people.

Free Church Presbytery

History turned an important page in the Hebrides when the Free Church Presbytery of Lewis met in the town of Stornoway. The Presbytery met to discuss the appalling spiritual conditions existing in their communities. No one for a moment dreamed how this special and providential meeting was destined to alter and shape history. We now know that this special meeting became the preliminary step to the amazing spiritual awakening that was to unfold.

The Free Church Presbytery expressed alarm and dismay that, while the places of entertainment were crowded, churches were almost empty. In many places youth had almost disappeared from the house of God. In fact at the parish of Barvas there was no longer a single young person attending public worship.[2] Church tradition had become unattractive to youth and even most adults. It was only a matter of time before many churches would have to close their doors if something did not change.

Free Church Presbytery of Lewis in Stornoway

Intercessors in Barvas

Among the people who were deeply concerned about the desperate spiritual conditions of the churches was a little group of seven men in the local parish of Barvas. This was the district that was to become the center of the outbreak of revival. These seven men were greatly burdened for revival for their community. So much so they committed themselves to meet several nights a week in an old thatched cottage serving as a storage "barn."[3] Here they met together night after night to intercede for God's intervention from heaven.

As they began praying, suddenly as a flash of light from heaven, they saw the truth that God is a covenant-keeping God. In Scripture it was clear to the men that God had given covenant promises to His people. "If this is true," they reasoned, "we can enter into a covenant with Him for our community. If we keep our part, then the covenant-keeping God must and will keep His." The question is: has God given a "covenant promise" for revival for us today?

As a direct answer to this question, these words were highlighted by the Holy Spirit to them:

If My people who are called by My name will humble themselves, and pray and seek My face, and turn from their wicked ways, then I will hear from heaven, and will forgive their sin and heal their land.[4]

Solemn Covenant

That night these men entered into a solemn covenant with God. They agreed to take upon themselves the "burden of the LORD" for revival in their community. Then they agreed together to humble themselves and to prevail in prayer until revival from heaven came.

Let us now go to that cottage-barn by the side of the road and see these men on their faces before God. They have gathered to pray, but this is no ordinary prayer meeting. Here are men, led by their minister, who are there to do business with God. At 10 o'clock at night they knelt down to plead with God that he would stretch forth His arm in revival.

For months they waited. Three nights a week they gathered in the old thatched cottage and waited before God in prayer until sometimes 4 or 5 o'clock in the morning. Like Jacob, they were determined to wrestle with God until the answer came. Then one night a young man, a deacon from the Free Church, arose from his knees and began to read Psalm 24—

Who shall ascend into the hill of the LORD? Or who may stand in His holy place? He who has clean hands and a pure heart, who has not lifted up his soul to an idol, nor sworn deceitfully. He shall receive blessing from the LORD....[5]

One elder then spoke: "Brethren, we have been praying for months for revival, waiting before God, but I would like to ask you now: Are our hands clean? Are our hearts pure?"

In response to this searching challenge, the men fell on their knees in confession and rededication to God. They again began to travail in prayer, even more earnestly. An hour later, three of the men were lying face down on the floor, having prayed until they were exhausted. By 5 A.M. breakthrough had begun! The place where they were praying was suddenly filled with the presence and glory of God! The power that God let loose in that little prayer meeting would eventually shake the entire island of Lewis.

That same morning, in a little cottage not far away, the two Smith sisters in their 80's were praying also. Having experienced revival in the past, they sought the face of God for revival in the present. They knew that others were waiting upon God that night. These two sisters, one was 84 and the other 82 years old, had huddled around their little peat fire to spend the night in prayer. Suddenly something happened! The presence and glory of God surged through their cottage.

Duncan Campbell

God spoke to the elderly Smith sisters, revealing to them the very man of God whom He was going to use in revival. This man's name was the Rev. Duncan Campbell, a Presbyterian minister from Scotland and a faithful man of prayer. God said: *In two weeks I shall send to this community the greatest spiritual awakening it has ever known.*

A telegram was sent to Duncan Campbell. HE WAS IN IRELAND AT THE TIME. He replied to the urgent telegram requesting his presence by saying that he was already scheduled for another meeting. His words were: *It is impossible for me to come at this time, but keep praying and I will come next year.*

When his reply came, the sisters responded with: *That is what man has said. God has said that he will be here in two weeks!*

Duncan Campbell with the elderly Smith sisters

In the meantime, other letters began to reach Duncan Campbell. The holiday conference that he was to address was suddenly canceled. Ireland's Touring Board unexpectedly swept in and commandeered both the hotels and boarding houses that Campbell's convention was depending on for its accommodations. Within two weeks Duncan Campbell arrived in Barvas. How amazingly God can overrule man's schedule.

The first scheduled revival service on the island of Lewis was held on 7th December 1949 in the old Barvas parish church. Many people had gathered in a great expectancy of a great "moving of God." Strangely enough, however, it was just an ordinary service. Seeing the disappointment on the preacher's face, one of the praying men came to him and said: *Don't be discouraged; it is coming. I already hear the rumbling of heaven's chariot wheels. We will have another night of prayer and then we will see what God is going to do.*

That night they about 30 people went to a nearby cottage where they knelt in prayer and began to travail before the Lord. At 3 o'clock in the morning, God swept in! About a dozen people were speechless as they lay on the floor. Something glorious had happened. God had begun to move into action as He had promised. Revival was at the door! Men and women were going to find deliverance.

When they left the place of prayer that morning, men and women everywhere were found seeking God. Lights burned in the homes along the road, as no one seemed to think of sleep. Three men, in a torment of conviction for their sins, were found lying by the roadside crying for God to have mercy on them. The

Spirit of God was moving into action, and the parish of Barvas on the island of Lewis was soon to be stirred from end to end.

NOTES

[1] Acts 1:14.

[2] From a taped message by Duncan Campbell, originally delivered to the students of the Faith Mission Bible College in Edinburgh, Scotland.

[3] Duncan Campbell mistakenly thought that the elders prayed in a "barn," because the old thatched cottage apparently was no longer lived in and possibly was being used for storage. Owen Murphy followed him in calling the thatched cottage a "barn" as have many other writers. See a picture of the thatched cottage where the elders prayed in the book by Colin and Mary Peckham, *Sounds from Heaven* (Ross-shire, Scotland: Christian Focus Publications, 2004), p. 128; see p. 103 for Peckham's correction.

[4] 2 Chronicles 7:14, NKJV

[5] Psalm 24:3-5a, NKJV.

What Does Revival Look Like?

John the Baptist appeared...,
preaching a baptism
of repentance for the forgiveness of sins.
The whole Judean countryside and
all the people of Jerusalem
went out to him.
—Mark 1:4-5

6

Scenes of the Supernatural

Two miles from Barvas in the village of Shader, on the 11th of December 1949, the spiritual awakening broke out during a Sunday evening service.[1] Shortly after the Shader service, the major spiritual explosion occurred at Barvas.

Those people who were privileged to attend the first services at Barvas will never forget them. People came from all four corners of the island on fourteen buses,[2] filling and crowding the church to overflowing. Seven men were being driven to the meeting in a butcher's truck, when suddenly the Spirit of God fell on them. In great conviction of sin all were converted before they even reached the church.

As the preacher delivered his message, tremendous conviction of sin swept over the people who had gathered both inside and outside this crowded building. Tears rolled down faces, and from every part of the building came the sounds of men and women crying out for mercy. So deep was their distress, their cries could be heard outside on the road. A young man up front at the altar near the pulpit cried out, "O God, hell is too good for me."

As the meeting closed and the people were leaving the building, inside a young man began to pray. He prayed under a tremendous burden of intercession for three-quarters of an hour. The people began to regather as he prayed, until there were twice as many outside the church as there were inside. When the young man stopped praying, the church elder had the people turn to

THE PARISH CHURCH OF BARVAS ON THE ISLAND OF LEWIS
This Parish Church was the epicenter of the Revival

Psalm 132. As the congregation sang Psalm 132, still more people streamed back into the church. This meeting continued into the morning hours.

The moment people took their seats, the Spirit of God began to sweep through the church. His presence brought powerful conviction of sin. Hardened sinners began to weep as well as to confess their sins.

Just as the meeting was closing, a messenger hurried up to the preacher, exclaiming, "Come with me. There's a crowd of people outside the police station. They are weeping and in awful distress. We don't know what's wrong with them. But they are calling for someone to come and pray for them."

When describing the scenes outside the police station, scenes that reminded one of the amazing days of Charles Finney and of the Welsh Revival, the minister declared:

I saw a sight I never thought was possible; something I shall never forget. Under a starlit sky, men and women were kneeling everywhere, by the roadside, outside the cottages, even behind the peat stacks, crying for God to have mercy upon them!

Hundreds of people had been making their way to the church when suddenly the Spirit of God had fallen upon them in great conviction of their sins. The weight of God's conviction for their sins caused them to fall to their knees in repentance, like Paul on the way to Damascus.

Revival Came To Arnol

For five weeks revival continued on and flourished in the villages of Barvas and Shader. Duncan Campbell conducted multiple services nightly, sometimes arriving home between 5 and 6 o'clock A.M. Nevertheless, he was very happy to be in the midst of such a wonderful moving of God.

After five weeks in one district, the revival began to spread. What had taken place in Barvas was now being repeated in other districts. As men and women throughout the island began to grip God in desperate intercession and prayer for revival, the Spirit of God swept on with increasing power.

A small community named Arnol came within the path of God's spiritual tornado. Gripped by a spirit of indifference about the church, seldom ever did a young person there attend a public service. The Sabbath was given over to drinking,[3] poaching,[4] and other sinful pleasures. When news reached Arnol that the gracious moving of God was spreading through the island, a meeting was held in opposition to the revival. Those attending this meeting clearly did not want such "religious things" coming to their town. Although the Arnol church was full in the first revival service, few people from Arnol were in attendance. The crowd that night was mainly from various other locations on the island.

In desperation for God to save Arnol, a little prayer band of men made their way to a farmhouse to plead the promises of God. Just after midnight, a young man rose to his feet and prayed the following prayer that will never be forgotten by those who were present:

Lord, You made a promise, are You going to fulfill it? We believe that You are a covenant-keeping God. Will You be true to Your covenant? You have said that You "will pour water upon him that is thirsty and floods upon the dry ground" [Isaiah 44:3, KJV]. Lord, I know how these ministers stand in Your presence, but if I know my own heart I know where I stand, and I tell Thee now that I am thirsty. Oh, I am thirsty for a manifestation of Your presence and power. And Lord, before I sit down, I want to tell You that Your honor is at stake!

This House Shook in Arnol in a Prayer Meeting during the Hebrides Revival

Have you ever prayed like that? Timid and cautious souls might believe that this prayer was not only audacious, but also presumptuous. Rather, however, here is a young man praying the prayer of faith that heaven must answer. One could imagine the angels of heaven looking over the walls of glory and saying: "This is a man who believes God. This is a man who dares to stand firm upon the promise of God and take from God what has been promised."

Then came the answer! There were individuals in Arnol who verified the fact that while this brother prayed, the farmhouse shook like a leaf. God, in agreement with this prayer, demonstrated His mighty power, just as He did in Acts 4:31. Dishes rattled upon the sideboard. An elder blurted out, "an earth tremor." Then wave after wave of divine power moved through the room.

Simultaneously, the Spirit of God also began moving through the village. People that night in Arnol could not sleep. Houses were lit all night. Some people walked the streets in great conviction of their sins. Others knelt beside their beds crying for God to pardon them.

As the praying men left the prayer meeting, the preacher walked into a house for a glass of milk and found the lady of the house, with seven others, down on their knees, crying for pardon. Arnol was being visited by the fire of God's presence. Fear of God and deep repentance were the consequence.

Within 48 hours the alcoholic drinking house, usually crowded with the drinking men of the village, was abandoned. Today it is in ruins. Fourteen young men who had been drinking there were gloriously converted. Those same men could be found three times a week, with others, down on their knees before God from 10 o'clock until after midnight, praying for their old associates, and for the spread of revival.

It was in this village also that within 48 hours nearly every young person between the ages of 12 and 20 had surrendered to Christ. And it was reckoned that every young man between the ages of 18 and 35 could be found in the prayer meetings.

The most notable convert at Arnol was a teenager age 16 named Donald MacPhail. God gave Donald immediately a supernatural anointing for praying. He became an outstanding intercessor and prayer warrior who came to be asked often to pray in the revival meetings in new and hard locations. One day Duncan Campbell found him in "the barn" with his Bible open. When interrupted, he quietly said: *Excuse me a little Mr Campbell, I'm having an audience with the King.*

The following is a testimony of Donald MacPhail compiled by Duncan Campbell from the Hebrides revival.

It was in the early spring of 1950, at the age of sixteen, that I found myself really gripped by fundamental thoughts which concerned the eternal welfare of my soul. I just wanted to be alone and contemplate. Often I took a walk across the moorland from our little village of Arnol on the Island of Lewis, and sometimes I caught myself crying as I sat down to watch and listen to the water running and rippling in the burn beside me.

"Why am I alive in this complicated world? Surely there must be a purpose in it all. Something inside me tells me that I am accountable for the life I live, and I am afraid: I cannot bear the thought which convinces me of a life after death." With heaviness, depression, and inward tension, these convictions captivated my simple mind.

At this time the news spread of a spiritual awakening down the coast in the villages of Barvas and Shadar. In the secondary school which I attended, boys and girls from these villages spoke of how a certain wild minister by the name of Duncan Campbell, preached fearlessly and forcibly, hitting and thumping the pulpits, and pointing his finger at people who automatically became infected with the 'coorum' – a term for conversion that seems to be considered by non-Christians in the Hebrides as a spiritual disease from which you may not recover. The next news I heard was that Mr. Campbell was to conduct a series of meetings in the mission hall [of Arnol].

As far as I could recollect, I had never attended the parish church, and to avoid 'spiritual infection' I had more or less decided I would not be seen within its walls. However, this was a chance not to be missed. Out of curiosity I attended the first meeting in order that I might know for myself whether what I heard was really the truth.

That very first night I was gripped by the Word read and preached, and could not stay away the following nights. Perhaps for the first time in my life I became aware of the presence of God, and began to understand something of my need of Christ as my Saviour from sin. From then on there followed days of secret struggle in prayer.

After a week of attending those meetings I could not resist the gospel call any longer. Vividly do I recall that dark Thursday night when the Word of God [reverberated] with conviction through my enlightened mind: I call heaven and earth to record this day against you, that I have set before you life and death, blessing and cursing: therefore choose life that both thou and thy seed may live (Deut. 30.19). With what clarity I saw and understood the way of salvation in Christ, yet at the same time I was given an insight into the terrible consequences of rejecting Christ, the Lord's provision for my salvation.

After the midnight cottage meeting I endeavored to leave for home, but on looking around, outside the house, I noticed a man praying by the side of the wall. Shouts and heavy sighs were heard from people within, as if crying for help. I could not restrain myself any longer and touched that godly man. In a broken voice I told him that I wanted to get right with God before it would be too late. As he turned, I saw Christ in the very expression on his face. In compassion he took me by the hand and led me into the prayer meeting where nine other villagers were on their knees, seeking the Saviour.

That night I was considerably relieved to have made a decision for Christ. At a subsequent prayer meeting, while a godly man from Shadar prayed, I became aware of the peace and joy of the Holy Spirit flooding my soul. I knew without doubt that my sins were forgiven. I confess with honesty that I had never known such deep peace, real joy, and inward liberty and freedom.

With considerable detail I could refer to other incidents [that] took place during the two following years on the Island of Lewis, of how we knew God's blessing in the meetings and saw many souls deciding for Christ.[5]

Donald MacPhail later attended Bible College and became a missionary to the Muslims in the modern Country of Yemen with the Church of Scotland Mission.

Duncan Campbell wrote this about Donald MacPhail:

Donald had a remarkable experience on the hillside a fortnight after he was born again. And God came upon him—the Holy Ghost came upon him. He had a mighty baptism in the Holy Spirit.

This 16-year-old fellow had such a baptism of God among the heather, that he forgot about coming home and a search party had to be sent out to find him in the hills. And they found him on his face among the heather repeating over and over, "Oh, Jesus, I love You. Oh, Jesus I love You." And wasn't he near to Jesus if he spoke like that? He was, of course.

One of the most outstanding anointings of prayer happened when Donald MacPhail was in Bernera. I was assisting at a communion service; the atmosphere was heavy and the preaching difficult, so I sent to Barvas for some men to come and assist in prayer. I also asked them to bring Donald MacPhail with them. And they prayed.

And now we are in the service in the church. And I am preaching from the text, "Who is this that cometh from Edom....this one that is glorious in his apparel, traveling in the greatness of his strength. I that speak in righteousness am mighty to save." That was the text. But oh, I tell you, the going was hard. The spiritual bondage persisted, so much so that half way through the sermon, I stopped preaching. I looked down and I saw little Donald sitting there, and I saw that his head was bowed and that the floor was wet with his tears. He was visibly moved under a deep burden for souls. I thought, "This boy is in touch with God, and living nearer to the Savior than I am."

And I stopped preaching. Looking down at this young lad, I said, "Donald, I believe God would have you lead us in prayer." That was right in the midst of my address. And that young lad stood to his feet.

Now that morning at family worship they were reading Revelation 4 where John has the vision of the open door. "I saw a door opened in heaven." And as that young man stood, that vision came before him. And this is what he said in his prayers: "God, I seem to be gazing in through *the open door. And I seem to see the Lamb standing in the midst of the throne. He has the keys of death and of hell on his belt." Then he stopped and began to weep. And for a minute or so, he wept and he wept. Oh, the brokenness. And when he was able to control himself, he lifted his eyes towards the heavens and he cried out, "God, there is power there, let it loose! Let it loose!"*

The Spirit of God swept into the building and the heavens were opened. The church resembled a battlefield. And now, one side of the church threw their hands up like this. Threw their heads back and you would almost declare that they were in an epileptic fit, but they were not. Oh, I can't explain it. And the other side they slumped on top of each other. But God, the Holy Ghost was moving in them. Those who had their hands like this stayed that way for two hours. [Now you try to remain like that with your hands up for a few minutes.] But you would break their hands before you could take them down. Now, I can't explain it, but that is what happened.

Another Difficult Location

In a town of Bernera things were much like Arnol. Bernera is a small island connected to Lewis by a bridge on the B8059. The Island of Bernera is approximately six miles long from North to south. The stream of spiritual life there was very low. Churches were empty and prayer meetings were practically nil. In view of this, a wire was sent to the praying men of Barvas to come and assist in prayer, and to bring with them Donald McPhail, the 16-year-old boy to whom God had imparted the amazing ministry of prayer. They came.

Halfway through the preacher's message, he stopped and called out, "Donald, will you lead us in prayer?" Standing to his feet, the teenager began to pour out his heart before God in agonizing intercession for the people of the island. Again he reminded God that He was the great "covenant-keeping God." Suddenly it seemed as though the heavens were rent and God swept through the church. People everywhere were stricken by the power of God, as the Spirit swept through the place in great convicting power.

Outside, startling things were taking place. Simultaneously, the Spirit of God had swept over the homes and area around the village, and everywhere people came under great conviction of sin. God gripped fishermen out in their boats, men behind their looms, men at the pit bank, a merchant out with his truck, and schoolteachers examining their papers. By 10 o'clock the roads were crowded with people, who streamed from every direction to the church.

As the preacher came out of the church, the Spirit of God swept among the people on the road as a wind. They gripped each other in fear. In agony of soul they trembled, many wept and some fell to the ground in great conviction of sin. Three men were found lying by the side of the road in such distress of soul that they could not even speak yet they had never been near the church!

So tremendous was the supernatural moving of God in conviction of sin, not a home, not a family, not an individual escaped fearful conviction, and even the routine of business was stopped that the island might seek the face of God like Nineveh in the days of Jonah. The town of Bernera was changed, lives and homes transformed, and even the fishing fleet, as it sailed out into the bays, took with it a "Presenter"[6] to lead them in prayer and singing of hymns.

Stornoway 1952

In January 1952, Duncan started a mission in Stornoway, the main town in Lewis. At first, things were very difficult, but after calling in reinforcements, in the second week, God broke through, and "they witnessed a mighty manifestation of the power of God. This was due to the young Donald MacPhail from Arnol. As he was praying, God swept in in power, and in a few minutes, some people were lying prostrate on the floor. The meeting continued till one o'clock in the morning.[7]

NOTES

[1] *Sounds from Heaven*, p. 76.

[2] From a taped message by Duncan Campbell, originally delivered to the students of the Faith Mission Bible College in Edinburgh, Scotland.

[3] Alcohol

[4] Poaching is hunting or fishing illegally

[5] This testimony of Donald MacPhail occurs in *Testimonies Compiled By Duncan Campbell From Hebrides Revival.* Transcribed from taped messages by Duncan Campbell.

[6] Lay minister

[7] Website of THE INTERCEDERS (Praying for Revival in Great Britain), "The Hebrides Revival and Awakening 1949-1953," in *The Interceders Encourager* No. 38.

Woe is me, for I am undone!
Because I am a man of unclean lips,
And I dwell in the midst of
a people of unclean lips;
For my eyes have seen the King,
the Lord of hosts.
—Isaiah 6:5 NKJV

7

Two Predominant Features

Revelation of God's holiness, accompanied by deep conviction among the people for personal sin, characterized the Hebrides revival.

1. Presence and Holiness

The fire of God's manifest presence and the revelation of His holiness were pervasive during the Hebrides revival. The supreme feature of this spiritual awakening was unquestionably the *deep consciousness of God's presence and holiness* that was everywhere evident among the people. People were so overwhelmed at times that they were afraid to open their mouths for fear that uttering careless words would bring upon them the judgments of God. Sinners, awed by an awareness of God's presence, would fall helplessly to the ground, crying out for His mercy. People were solemnly subdued and walked quietly before God. As in every true revival, *the shop became a pulpit, the home a sanctuary, and the heart an altar.*

2. Conviction of Sin

In any revival where there is a manifestation of the fire of God's presence and holiness, there will also be an intense awareness and conviction of sin in saints and sinners alike. This without a doubt was also a predominant feature of the Hebrides' visitation. A visiting minister from Lewis declared: *So tremendous has been this sense of an "awareness of God" that I have known men out in the fields, others at their [weaving] looms, so overcome that they were prostrate upon the ground.*

One notable example of the grace of God was that of an individual who was saved while crossing a field. This person's testimony was: *So awesome and pervasive was the sense of God's presence that even the grass beneath my feet and the rocks around me seemed to cry out "flee to Christ for refuge."*

So intense was the pervasive conviction of sin in the district that even the toughest, most hardened and most notorious sinners literally cried out in agony of soul. Some were found lying helpless by the roadsides, stricken with conviction as in the days of Wesley, Finney, and the Welsh Revival.

Another remarkable feature of the Hebrides revival was the persistent way the Holy Spirit pursued men and women until they repented of their sins and were soundly converted. Such was the case of a young man.

Like Jonah in the Old Testament, he discovered that it is impossible to escape from God. One night, after being spoken to about his personal need of salvation, conviction suddenly gripped him and he began to tremble. *"This won't get hold of me,"* he muttered. *"I'll get away from here and drink my way out of it."*

When entering the drinking house, to his consternation, he overheard a group of men discussing their own great conviction of sin and fear of being lost. He trembled even more, *"This is no place for a man who wants to shake this off,"* he muttered. *"I'll go over to the dance hall and I'll dance my way out of it."* He had not been in the dance hall very long before a young lady came up to him, exclaiming, *"Oh, where would eternity find us, if God should strike us dead tonight?"* Tremendous conviction swept over this young man and he surrendered himself to Christ.

So widespread was the conviction of sin that in some districts hardly a person escaped. A man who had very little time for God was one day driving along the road when suddenly he saw before him a vision of hell. Startled, he jammed on his brakes, pulled the car to the roadside, then kneeling beside the car, he surrendered to Christ.

Sometimes conviction rested upon sinners for days. The Holy Spirit's conviction would cause sinners great distress of mind and heart. Such was the case of one particular man. So convinced was he of his godless life and his seeming inability to get peace of mind in spite of repentance, he rushed down to the seashore. Hiding among the rocks, he prepared to commit suicide. A young woman, while praying, had a vision of this man. God showed her exactly where he was and what he was about to do. Quickly rising to her feet, she called her minister and instructed him where to find the tormented man. The minister arrived just in time to save the man's life, not only from physical death but also from an eternal hell.

Another example of great conviction of sin was that of a man working in the fields. He later became a wonderful trophy of God's grace. While working out in the fields, great conviction fell on him. He began to tremble violently. *"You're not a sissy,"* he said to himself, *"what's the matter with you?"* The voice of God seemed to thunder into his soul. *"You are a poacher and a Sabbath breaker."* He knew what God meant. He had been breaking the law by poaching. He was a drunkard also, a real godless fellow, and this was a new experience for him. Feeling miserable and wretched because of his sin and guilt, he went to the church and was gloriously converted.

God confronted another man in the same amazing way while he was sitting in a guesthouse. As he was reaching to pick up his beer, he became suddenly conscious of the presence of God. He began to tremble. Great conviction took hold of him as the voice of God began to thunder in his soul. Putting down his beer, he repented of his drinking habit. Shortly afterwards, he was gloriously converted and became a real witness for God.

This is revival from heaven! The supernatural power of God gripped the hearts of men in soul-shaking conviction of sin! Many who encountered this pervasive manifestation of God were smitten with conviction and left helpless when they went down under the power of God. Others cried out in agony of mind and repentance for days before coming to peace with God. Such is the amazing heart searching conviction that comes from a genuine visitation of God from heaven. It was both terrifying and glorious to behold.

Oh, sing to the Lord a new song!
For He has done marvelous things;
His right hand and His holy arm
have gained Him
the victory.
—Psalm 98:1 NKJV

8

Effects of God's Fiery Visitation

What lasting effects did the revival have in the various districts of the Hebrides? As in all revivals there were some geographical areas that were not greatly impacted for one reason or another. On the other hand, there were areas where the fruit of revival was lasting and involved profound transformation. Many young people who were saved during the revival became full time ministers and/or missionaries.[1]

Contagious Fire

History records that multiplied thousands of people came face to face with God during the great New York City "Prayer Meeting Revival" of 1857-59. The spiritual awakenings that reverberated from it, like shock waves, spread to one American city after another. In the streets, in homes, as well as in the churches, people were smitten with deep conviction of sin and in their great soul distress found salvation. Taverns lost their regular customers, family altars were restored, marriages and families were reunited, social evils disappeared, and churches found new life.

In the mighty manifestation of God in 1904, when the Holy Spirit and revival swept through the land of Wales, similar scenes were reported. A clipping from the local newspaper declared:

Infidels have been converted; drunkards, gamblers, thieves, saved; and many thousands have been reclaimed to respectability and honored citizenship. Confessions of awful sins have been heard, old debts have been paid, theatres and beer saloons in distress for lack of patronage. Several police courts have become completely idle. In five weeks, 20,000 conversions have been reported.

Such were the proofs and fruit of revival in the wonderful days of the Welsh revival.

The blessing of the Lord in the Hebrides was on a smaller population scale and localized to certain districts. Nevertheless, it bore the hallmark of a similar "supernatural moving of God." Subsequently, the revival inspired and challenged leaders and intercessors far and wide to seek God for far greater things.

Revival Impact

What impact did the revival have on the church and community? In his message at the Keswick Convention in 1952, Duncan Campbell declared that because of the Hebrides revival,

More people are attending prayer meetings in Lewis today, than attended public worship on the Sabbath [day] before the outbreak of this revival. That is the impact on the church; but what about this community? I make this statement: Social evils were swept away as by a flood in the night, and in the communities touched by this gracious movement you have men and women living for God. Family worship [can be found] in every home, five or six prayer meetings [occur each] week in the parish; the ministers and elders [are] doing their utmost to build up the young men and women in the faith .... Of the hundreds that professed [i.e., who turned to Christ] during this gracious first wave of the Holy Spirit, right up to my visit to this particular district, only four young women have ceased to attend the prayer meetings. Only four of the hundreds that came to know Jesus Christ.[2]

In nearly every home of some districts, one could find families regularly praying and reading the Scriptures together. Prayer meetings were better attended than the public meetings were before the revival! Converts came to be numbered by their attendance at the prayer meetings. Absence from the prayer meeting meant a "doubted conversion." Here is a standard, apart from revival, that very few churches would dare to adopt! If we judged our converts, or even our membership by attendance at the prayer meetings, what would happen?

A New Song

One remarkable characteristic of the Hebrides revival is the fact that over 80 new spiritual songs or hymns were written. In spite of the manifestation of God's presence and holiness in fearful conviction of sin and judgment, almost every song written during the revival had for its theme "the love of God."

Singing the Scriptures was an outstanding feature of the revival. "The singing was like fire" that went right through a person's whole being. The singing was *almost supernatural, full of joy and spiritual power.*[3] People sang everywhere: on public transport, on buses coming to and returning from public services, on the streets, in house meetings, etc.[4]

Community Transformation

Communities, homes, and churches were all impacted by the revival. Even the realm of politics came under its influence, as did every area of community life. The following is a noteworthy example. During the revival a crowd of people had gathered to listen to one of the leading socialists, but he failed to make his appearance. Searching everywhere, his associates at last found him beside his bed in prayer. *What's the meaning of this?* they demanded. *Don't you know the people are waiting to hear you speak to them?*

Turning a tear-stained face to them, he replied: *Go back and tell them I have business with God. And if any of them know how to pray, tell them to pray for me because I really need it!* The announcement was made at the political rally with such impressive results that the meeting broke up in confusion.

Years later in the Hebrides, there were hundreds of men and women who were among the happiest on the islands. They were the men and women whose lives had been changed by Christ and had been given a new beginning. Because of God's manifest presence in this gracious revival, they had made the discovery of a lifetime.

They discovered the reality of God! Likewise, they discovered the great things He had been waiting to do for them! They were miracles of God's redeeming love. They had new homes, new lives, and they lived in a new world of peace and happiness. The changed lives and homes, and the transformed churches and communities from the Hebrides revival are historical proof of the tremendous potential and transforming power bound up in an historic revival from heaven.

NOTES

[1] From a taped message by Duncan Campbell, originally delivered to the students of the Faith Mission Bible College in Edinburgh, Scotland.

[2] Duncan Campbell's Keswick message on Friday, 18 July 1952, printed in *The Keswick Week* magazine (1952), pg. 147.

[3] *Sounds from Heaven*, pg. 93.

[4] Ibid., pg. 95

Because your heart was tender
and you humbled yourself before God
when you heard his words
against this place and its inhabitants,
and you have humbled yourself before Me
and have torn your clothes and wept
before Me,
I also have heard you,
declares the Lord.
—2 Chronicles 34:27 ESV

9

What Made the Revival Possible?

The Hebrides revival was truly a public manifestation of God's presence. Greater than organization, more wonderful than a new approach in dynamic evangelism, this was God Himself in action! The magnetism of His awesome presence worked independently of special personalities. Behind this "turning loose" of the almost irresistible power of God, was a divinely inspired strategy.

This strategy was simple but profound: one minister and seven elders praying in an old thatched cottage by the side of the road. These men were prepared *to stand in the gap*[1] and to pay the full price that God requires in order for revival to come.

These men were characterized by three essential intercessory principles that always move the heart of God.

1. Faith in a "Covenant-Keeping" God

These were men who believed that revival was possible for their church and community because of the covenant promises of God. These men, like the Psalmist, trusted God according to His Word (Psalm 119). Had not God declared:

If My people who are called by My name will humble themselves, and pray and seek My face, and turn from their wicked ways, then I will hear from heaven, and will forgive their sin and heal their land.[2]

A covenant is a binding "agreement" on both parties. Since God is a covenant-making and covenant-keeping God, then this promise must be as binding on Him as it is on us. If we fulfill our part of the covenant, then He must fulfill His. If God is God, then He is true. If He is truthful and trustworthy, then His word must come to pass and we can absolutely depend upon it.

God has established a covenant agreement in 2 Chronicles 7:14 that relates to revival; He is waiting to send it. Since this is true, revival does not depend on God alone, but also on His people meeting the conditions of the covenant. Staking everything upon this fact, three times each week the elders met in the old cottage to keep the "conditions" of the covenant promise. They were confident that their covenant-keeping God would stand by His promise and hear from heaven.

Each night as these men prayed, they would renew their faith by remembering God's promise. In absolute confidence in God's faithfulness, they declared before the presence of God the certainty of the coming revival. Nothing, including the weary months of waiting without their "answer," could weaken their confidence in the fact that their God, a covenant-keeping God, would fulfill His promise.

2. Humility Before God

If my people ... will humble themselves. God is holy, and humanity must humble itself before deity. Before we can stand upon holy ground, we must be clean. Watch the drama in the old thatched cottage unfold itself as one of the men slowly rises from his knees, takes up the Word and begins to read from Psalm 24:

Who may ascend into the hill of the Lord? Or who may stand in His holy place? He who has clean hands and a pure heart, who has not lifted up his soul to an idol, nor sworn deceitfully. He shall receive blessing from the Lord.[3]

As words of fire falling from the lips of a Holy God, every word seemed to burn its way into the very depths of the hearts of the men who gathered to do business with God. In view of the tremendous challenge of this declaration, these elders unhesitatingly went to their knees in unreserved surrender and dedication to God. Here were men who were prepared to meet every demand of God that revival might come, whatever the personal cost might be. That price, which has never varied through the ages, is brokenness before God and the emptying of "self" in all its manifestations. Emptying of self includes a forsaking of all sin and sinful "habits," and a total surrender to God and His purposes.

3. Travailing and Prevailing Prayer

God is always searching for a people who will humble themselves to pray, intercede and travail before Him for revival. Such a people He found on the island of Lewis in the Hebrides.

And how they prayed! Their prayers were not the half-hearted, sentimental, churchy, double-minded prayers to which we are accustomed today and that accomplish so little. As these men literally wrestled with God, they entered into the spiritual conflict with every bit of power and energy they possessed. Their prayer was like the prayer of the Master as in Gethsemane, *Who, in the days of His flesh . . . offered up prayers and supplications with vehement cries and tears. . . .*[4]

The elders at Barvas in the Hebrides, who had covenanted to stand in the gap for revival, prayed consistently, persistently and earnestly like Elijah. In desperation they stormed the throne-room of God. Burning passion, concern for the lost, and absolute confidence in God, based on the blood of Jesus, gripped every word that fell from their praying lips. They prayed until they lay helpless and exhausted. What depths of reaching out to God! They prayed until they travailed; they travailed until they prevailed. They prayed until God answered from heaven. Travail must always precede prevail. *When Zion travailed she brought forth.*[5]

NOTES

[1] Ezekiel 22:30

[2] 2 Chronicles 7:14, NKJV

[3] Psalm 24:3-5a, NKJV

[4] Hebrews 5:7, NKJV.

[5] Isaiah 66:8

*If My people
who are called by My name
will humble themselves,
and pray
and seek My face,
and turn from their wicked ways,
then I will hear from heaven....
—2 Chronicles 7:14 NKJV*

10

The Enduring Challenge

As one of the most stirring events of the mid-twentieth century, God's visitation to the Hebrides represents a great spiritual challenge for this generation in the twenty-first century. This amazing revival reveals the tremendous potential of a genuine outpouring of the Holy Spirit for all churches and communities. The pattern of events that led up to this Hebridean revival, amplified by the declarations of God's Word, makes it very evident that what took place in the Hebrides can be experienced here in America or elsewhere. The covenant promise of 2 Chronicles 7:14 is just as applicable to America as to any other part of the earth.

Challenge for Spiritual Leaders

The challenge of the Hebrides is one for every minister of the gospel. Gathered with the seven elders in the Hebridean cottage was their spiritual leader, representing every spiritual leader who is prepared to join with his or her people in seeking the face of God for revival from heaven.

Standing in the shadows behind the revival was another man of God, Duncan Campbell. He was to be God's chosen servant and spokesman for the revival. Duncan Campbell stands as a challenge to every minister of the gospel to be devoted to prayer and the Word, a consecrated and holy vessel of the Lord, and prepared for the Master's chosen purpose.

Burdened because of the spiritual indifference of the ungodly, grieved at the decline of spiritual life in the churches, and feeling utterly helpless in the face of such a challenge, Duncan Campbell knelt in his study crying out to God. Suddenly, but quietly, the Spirit of the Lord came upon him. Before him appeared a vision of a dying world plunging into an abyss of eternal darkness, and multitudes of men and women speeding on to Christless graves. Then came the great realization that was to transform his ministry. He saw that God was not only God, but also a covenant-keeping God who has made covenant promises to His people.

Like a flash of light he suddenly saw that there was a great realm of potential power and blessing within his grasp through the covenant promises of God. He personally could enter into a covenant with God. If he were prepared to pay the price, he could have more of the moving of the Spirit of God in his ministry than he had ever known before. From that moment, through complete surrender to the Lord and constant waiting before God, Duncan Campbell entered into a ministry that caused men and women to feel the impact of God's holy presence.

Through his fearless preaching on the judgments of God against sin, and his emphasis on the faithfulness of a covenant-keeping God, hundreds of people, stricken by the most severe conviction of sin, turned to God. This kind of ministry is needed desperately today. Ministry that is similarly empowered by the Holy Spirit will produce hunger for God and serious conviction of sin. Spirit-empowered preaching will break the deception of the multitudes so that they can turn in true repentance and faith to Christ.

Lukewarm, unimpassioned preaching has never raised the dead, physically or spiritually! Only passionate preaching with a demonstration of the Holy Spirit's power will do that! In the days of Whitefield and Wesley it was a common sight for sinners to "cry out as in the agony of death." History records that under Whitefield's anointed preaching, so great was the conviction of sin that some were "struck pale as death" and fell to the ground. Others, sinking into the arms of their friends lifted up their eyes to heaven, crying out for mercy.

During the great Scottish Revival in 1850, James Turner, the fiery Methodist preacher, went down to Pontrochie to preach. So great was the conviction of sin that many businesses had to close down temporarily in order that the people might get right with God.

Meetings lasted from 14 to 18 hours. Sinners, hearing about their lost condition, literally went down and out under God's power. Afterwards they came up praising God for His forgiveness and acceptance.

Among the spiritual giants of former American evangelism was John Wesley Redfield, a man sent from God, whose ministry was filled with the Holy Spirit's power and conviction. Redfield was born in New Hampshire in 1810. In his early years, while kneeling under a large tree in the heart of a forest, he accepted Christ as his Savior. In subsequent years as a preacher of the gospel, so tremendous was the moving of God in his ministry that multitudes found Christ. On one occasion, after weeping before God, he heard God speak to him: *You may prepare for the greatest display of God's power that you have ever witnessed in this church!*

That night before Redfield finished his sermon, people crying out for mercy flocked to the altars. On another occasion, the church was suddenly filled with a terrifying sense of the fire of God's presence. Then, like a thunderclap, the power of God broke out in the meeting and hundreds, panic-stricken with the fear of God, crowded the altars begging God to have mercy on them.

Great manifestations of power were widespread. Persons would flee from their homes attempting to avoid yielding to Christ, and afterwards be found lying helpless by the roadside. Eventually found by the police, they were taken to the station house and placed on the floor where they were watched until they "came to."

During the Second Great Awakening revival at Yale University and New Haven (Connecticut), so intense was the conviction of sin that in some meetings the entire gathering numbering hundreds of people were stricken by the power of God.

Certainly secular humanism is eroding faith in the Western world today. Is it not true also that passionless, lukewarm churches and Christians are subtly destroying true faith and making it seem irrelevant? The answer is a resounding "yes"! We need another visitation of God, Fire and Revival from heaven that brings revelation of God's holiness and the deceptive destructiveness of sin. Only such a visitation will be accompanied by sin-convicting power and the fear of the LORD. Only such a visitation will revitalize both spiritual leaders and their congregations. Only such a visitation in spiritual awakening of sinners will cause them to turn wholeheartedly from their sinful lifestyles to Christ in authentic repentance and faith.

This is the ministry God is waiting to send to America. This is the ministry that the great God of revival is waiting to impart to those who will seek His face and presence in fasting and prayer. Spiritual leaders who are determined to do so "until" there is a God-encounter, will be faithfully met by Him in a fresh experience of His presence and power. Only then can those preachers of the gospel go forth fearlessly, proclaiming the whole counsel of God including the judgments of God.

The very prospect of such a visitation of God will disturb and disrupt many spiritual leaders who have been content with a prayerless and powerless ministry. Ministry that is based solely on theology without the manifest power of God will be greatly challenged. Ministers, who have been so cautious about God's manifest power that they have gone into spiritual stagnation, applies to many of us in varying degrees. Most western spiritual leaders, if they are to receive the manifest power of God as in the Hebrides, will have to revise much of their thinking. The revival in the Hebrides illustrates clearly that where there is the visitation of God's fiery presence, there often will be unusual manifestations of His power. And those unusual manifestations are neither hype nor emotionalism.

None of us want to embrace religious fanaticism or fleshly demonstrations. But neither can we afford to confuse these with the unusual manifestations that are the direct result of the genuine activity of the Holy Spirit. If one removes the so-called sensational scenes and supernatural manifestations from such revivals as those of Wesley, Finney and the 1904 Welsh revival, then what remains is not revival.

Fear of unusual manifestations has been a prominent hindrance to revival for generations in

Western Christianity. This is generally true both among ministers and churches alike. The great moving of God in the Hebrides is a challenge to us all to face the issue honestly and fearlessly. What exactly does God have to say concerning this? From an honest study of the Word of God, these facts are evident:

1. Unusual Manifestations of the Spirit Are Unrelated to Spiritual Hype or Fleshly Emotion

There are unusual manifestations that emanate from the supernatural operation of God. God is sensational because God is supernatural. When He spoke, creation came into being. Was that not sensational? *Even the morning stars sang together*[1] in worship and wonder at the mighty act of creation. Every miracle of God in both the Old and New Testament days was sensational in the eyes of men. When the waters of the Red Sea parted in response to Moses' staff, when the sun stood still in the days of Joshua, when the fire fell from heaven in the days of Elijah, were these acts not unusual, even "sensational manifestations?"

When Jesus healed the sick and raised the dead, when Peter and John brought healing to the lame man at the Temple gate, when the Spirit of God was poured out on 120 of Jesus' disciples in Jerusalem on the Day of Pentecost, causing thousands to be converted, were these acts not unusual? Did these not cause sensational awe of God?

Certainly they did! Yet these acts were not "fanaticism." These were the acts of a miracle-working God manifesting His divine power in order that the eyes of the people might be turned to Him. The Word of God, and the manifestations of God throughout history, emphasize the fact that where there is a genuine "moving of God," there will also be unusual manifestations of God. When real revival comes, this fact needs to be clear in our minds and hearts. There are "worked-up" acts of men that are "fanaticism," but the acts of God are "sensational." And God's personality and nature have not and will not change!

2. Fear of Unusual Manifestations or Unbelief About the Supernatural Can Hinder Revival and the Ministry of the Holy Spirit

Humankind today is still only probing the "fringe" of the tremendous potential of the realm of FAITH. Nevertheless, one startling and tremendous fact is obvious: God will only work where there is earnest intercession and genuine faith. Where there is UNBELIEF, God waits until intercession and faith arise.

The prophetic cry in the Old Testament was: you have limited the Holy One of Israel.[2] The New Testament testifies about Jesus' ministry at Nazareth that He did not do many mighty works there because of their unbelief.[3]

Shall we be guilty of the same act of unbelief through our "fear" about God working in an unfamiliar way? We thrill at the very reading of the mighty acts of God in the days of Moses, Joshua, Elijah, Elisha, and the New Testament Apostles. But what would have happened if they had doubted and limited God? The biblical answer is, "nothing"!

If "fear" of unusual manifestations had gripped their hearts, there would never have been the parting of the waters of the Red Sea, nor the crumbling walls of Jericho, nor the fire falling from heaven on Mt. Carmel, nor the mighty miracles of Jesus' Apostles. These mighty men of Bible days would never have dared to obey the commands of God that made it possible for these amazing events to take place.

This lesson is equally true and applicable today. If we truly desire a genuine revival in our generation and community, we must shed our self-imposed fears. We do this by humbling ourselves before God and by permitting Him to operate according to His own prerogative. There is no "fanaticism" in the real activity of God, but there will be unusual manifestations of God's majesty and works at which multitudes will marvel.

Are we, then, prepared to receive such a ministry of God's Spirit and power? If so, the price of God's power and revival visitation have not changed. See Duncan Campbell in his office on his face before God. See that life utterly dedicated to God and His work. Listen to the travail of his soul as he cries out to God, even until the early hours of the morning. See the floor wet with his tears. *Here is the price* for life and conviction in ministry! Then see those towns swept by the fire of God's presence and power. See those lives, homes and communities transformed by the grace of God. *Here is the reward* for those who will pay the price. Such is the tremendous challenge of revival for every spiritual leader.

Challenge to the Churches

The church and our cities in the Western world desperately need revival. The church, like a mammoth organization, has everything except the manifest presence and mighty power of God. As someone has said: "We have equipment but not enduement; commotion but not creation; action but not unction; rattle but not revival." We tend to equate spirituality with church activity. If we really desire true revival, we must seriously get down to business with God.

As with the Hebridean elders of Barvas, we must be prepared to accept the burden for revival as our own personal responsibility and solemnly covenant with God on the basis of His covenant promise in 2 Chronicles 7:14. The binding conditions of this agreement demand first of all a *humbling of ourselves* that we may have *clean hands and pure hearts* and thereby be able to *stand in his holy place.*[4]

This requires the confession of every sin, a turning away from all that is unrighteous, a forsaking of every doubtful habit, and an utter surrender to Christ. Revival, in the sense of God's holy presence and glory among us, must be the dominating desire of life. For many people it will mean the giving up of idols that they have cherished for years. For others it may mean a visit to the "tents" as in the days of Achan to unearth some of the things hidden there. It may be a "wedge of gold" or a "Babylonian garment" or some of the "spoils of battle" that have to go before the blessings of the Lord can come.

One thing is very certain whatever the finger of God points to as wrong in our lives, those things must go. Seven men, travailing before God for five lonely months, were not enough to bring revival. Before a covenant-keeping God would answer and fulfill His promise, these men had to completely fulfill the conditions of the covenant.

They had to humble themselves before Almighty God and turn from their wicked ways. There was not only God's request for *clean hands and pure hearts*, but also the experience of it was required. This came for them only by personal confession of all sin and complete, unreserved surrender of all areas of their lives to Christ.

Then God required not only prayer, but also prevailing prayer. Prevailing prayer begins in travail and continues in travail until the answer comes. Churches with no weeping, no confessing of sin and no prayer or fasting do not have Hebridean like visitations from on high. In the days of the prophet Ezekiel, did God not say to the man with the inkhorn by his side: *Go through the midst of the city ... and put a mark on the foreheads of the men who sigh and cry over all the abominations that are done within it.*[5]

What God is seeking for today is not a people with an outward sign of religion and respectability, nor even preachers whose names are known nationwide. Rather, God is looking for those whose hearts are burdened and broken, and whose eyes are red with weeping before Him because of the sins and abominations of the cities. Weeping in both the pulpit and the pew is the necessary price for visitations from on high.

Nations stand at the crossroads of destiny, faced with an unavoidable choice: the mark of the man with the inkhorn or the mark of the beast! The alternative is a Christ-centered revival through a people who are on their faces before God, or an anti-Christ apostasy. Unless there are tears of intercession by God's people and spiritual leaders, there will be tears in the streets, schools and homes.

Already Western nations stagger beneath gigantic burdens of spiritual lukewarmness, moral erosion, materialistic idolatry and blatant immorality with multiplied thousands of demoralized lives, marriages and homes. Added to this is the evergrowing threat of nations being over-run by humanism and lawlessness that can ultimately plunge a nation into indescribable chaos resulting in riots, fear, a breakdown in civility and millions being killed through terrorist invasions, plagues and war.

In view of these sobering facts, what is the verdict of the "man with the inkhorn" as he passes our way? Is the "mark" upon our foreheads? The price is heavy, but as President Eisenhower of America once declared: "A soldier's pack may be heavy, but it is lighter than a prisoner's chains." How much better to pay the price for revival from heaven than to wear the prisoner's shackles of sin's consequences in a nation.

Abraham stood before the Lord and interceded for godless Sodom until God's mercy was exhausted. Elijah stood before God for backslidden Israel until fire fell from heaven, the altars of Baal were broken down and many turned to God. Down through the centuries individuals have dared to stand before God in holy desperation for the sins of their generation until God has moved out of His Holy Temple in nation-shaking revival.

We treasure the memories of the great men and women of God from days gone by who have caused multitudes to turn to Christ, and whose God-anointed exploits are recorded in history. When we think of such men as John Wesley, George Whitefield, Charles Finney, and Evan Roberts, we revere their memories, build memorials, and sing their praises. We do everything but imitate them! Each of these men could have pointed to a sacred place by his bedside that was wet with tears of intercession. These men often prayed in such travail of soul that they lay exhausted in a pool of tears.

David Brainerd prayed in such agony of soul for the American Indians in Massachusetts that his body became abnormally affected. But he saw revival! John Knox, whose prayers shook Scotland, was so desperate in prayer that to see him on his knees was a sight that inspired awe. And he saw spiritual awakening! George Fox so connected with God in travailing prayer that men were often afraid to look on his face as he came out of his prayer chamber. And a Spirit-filled movement was birthed!

The half-hearted prayer meetings of today are a mockery in comparison to the depth of spiritual travail of such people who, in days gone by, caused nations to be swept by the power of God. The price for heaven-sent revival has never changed. Before the floods of Holy Spirit conviction could sweep across the Isles of the Hebrides, strong men had to be broken before God. Upon their faces before God, people had to travail in agony of prayer through the long hours of the night for months. To do this, in spite of the demands of home and work, these men had to make time for waiting before God.

Outpourings from on high must be preceded by a willingness to make time to wait upon God. This is perhaps the greatest problem before us today. We have all the modern luxuries of life to make work easier and yet we cannot make time to pray. What a tragic paradox! Dr. Wilbur Smith very aptly stated the problem when he said: "I never get time to pray; I've always got to make it!"

The floodtides of revival are waiting to be released upon the face of the earth. God's covenant promise is a guarantee of this. But before the floodgates can be opened, we must make time to wait before God. And in that waiting before Him there must be travailing and prevailing prayer. Regardless of the godless world outside, regardless of the many who are indifferent and the very few who will stand with us, like the praying men of the Hebrides who emptied themselves, we must throw every bit of our energy into desperate travailing intercession. Moreover, the intercession must continue until God hears from heaven and our nations are swept by the burning cleansing flame of a Holy Spirit revival.

Are we prepared to face this challenge? Dare we honestly enter into such a covenant with God? If we do, then here are the covenant conditions laid down by God as the price we will have to pay.

Conditions of Revival Covenant (2 Chronicles 7:14)

1. Humbling: "If my people will humble themselves …"

This will consist of humbling oneself before God, before others and before self. Included in this process will be deep, honest, heart searching, heart confession, turning from sin, forsaking sinful and hurtful habits, making restitution for wrong doings, and committing to a complete dedication of ourselves to God and His work.

2. Praying: "…and pray,"

By resolute faith in the certainty that God will keep His promise, by travailing before God in earnest prayer, by ever declaring before Him His covenant promise, we must pray UNTIL we receive what was promised. The effectiveness of your praying will not depend upon the amount of support received from others who join you, neither will it be diminished by those who refuse to join you. Its basis will be the solid fact of God's covenant promise that "if we will… then He will hear from heaven."

3. Seeking: "…and seek My face,"

God promises elsewhere, *You will. . .seek me and find me when you seek me with all your heart.*[6] Seeking Him with an undivided heart is focused abandonment, giving Him full attention. Nowhere does God say: seek Me but sometimes it will be in vain. That is Satan's lie. Seeking God is never for nothing! The reward of seeking His face is finding Him.[7]

4. Turning: "...and turn from their wicked ways."

Before there can be dedication, there must be renunciation. To have *clean hands and pure hearts,*[8] there must be a *turning-away* from anything that would contaminate or defile spiritual life. God is in His HOLY TEMPLE. To approach Him we must stand on HOLY GROUND. To do this we must be HOLY PEOPLE.

It is here where the real heart-searching must take place. There are many things that represent *wicked ways* in the eyes of God that are perhaps held very lightly in our estimation. It is easy to fall into Achan's sin of touching what is forbidden! *The shekels of silver, the wedge of gold and the Babylonian garment*[9] make strong appeals to the *flesh.* It is often very easy to yield to these desires, bring them into the "tent" and then cover them up by making excuses to our own conscience.

The stark fact is that there is nothing hidden from the eyes of Him with whom we have to do. We may cover things up from the eyes of our friends, but nothing is hidden from God. The blessing of God may well depend not only on a clean life, but also a clean dwelling place. There may be contaminating "idols" in the home that will have to go before we have completely *turned from our wicked ways.*[10] Are we prepared to do that? Are we prepared to wait before God in an honest heart-searching posture until He has revealed every *wicked way*[11] that would hinder us? Are we then prepared to decisively turn from them, whatever the sacrifice involved, by the grace of God?

Then, and only then, shall we stand on covenant ground, and hear the mighty God of Bible days declare: *Call to me, and I will answer you, and show you great and mighty things, which you do not know!*[12] Only then shall we SEE Him move into action in the greatest spiritual awakening that the American continent has ever experienced!

The following challenging words from the *Keswick Week Magazine* (1952) are a fitting conclusion to this chapter:

We may organize, we may plan, but until we get on our faces before God and do business with a covenant-keeping God, we shall not see revival. We can have our conventions and conferences, and speak of our wonderful times, but what we want and what we need is a fresh manifestation of the mighty power of God that brings men down in deep conviction to seek the Saviour.[13]

NOTES

[1] Job 38:7

[2] Psalm 78:41

[3] Matthew 13:58

[4] Psalm 24:3-4

[5] Ezekiel 9:4

[6] Jer. 29:13

[7] cf. Heb. 11:6

[8] Psalm 24:4

[9] Joshua 7:24

[10] 2 Chronicles 7:14

[11] Psalm 139:23-24

[12] Jeremiah 33:3

[13] *The Keswick Week* magazine (1952), pg. 147.

If My people will. . . , then I will....
Now My eyes will be open and
My ears attentive to
prayer made in this place.
—2 Chronicles 7:14-15 NKJV

11

The Power of Covenant Prayer

The power of covenant prayer is a biblical truth that has transformed the prayer-life of many believers the world over. It will also light the fires of revival, and lead multitudes into a new realm of spiritual authority and answers to prayer from God.

The rising tide of spiritual power that is sweeping across the face of the earth has demonstrated that God's people can enter into a solemn covenant with Him based on the clear promises of His Word. Then through serious faith-filled covenant prayer, they can become recipients of God's power and blessing such as they have never known before.

What Is "Covenant Prayer"?

In the ancient world when two tribal chiefs chose to enter into a covenant with each other, they would each cut a vein in the other's arm to cause the blood to flow. Afterwards they would put one person's arm to the other's arm to "mingle their blood" and then each one would drink. From that moment they regarded themselves as bound together by an indissoluble bond, stronger than any earthly tie. To prove their unity of agreement and bond together, they would blend their names, as God did with Abraham when He took the letter "H" out of His own name and added it to Abram's, saying: *No longer shall your name be called Abram, but your name shall be Abraham.*[1]

Such a covenant was of tremendous value for a smaller tribe. From that moment onwards it had the right to the power and prestige and resources of its more powerful "covenant" friend. When attacked by an enemy, the smaller tribe's greatest weapon was to cry aloud the mighty name it now bore! Enemies knew that the one who was called upon would immediately respond and come to the other's aid. The enemy no longer faced a small tribe but the mighty forces of the powerful tribe with which the smaller had entered into covenant relationship.

When the covenant was made, the more powerful chief would lay down conditions that the smaller tribe was obligated to obey implicitly. In turn the smaller tribe had the right to call upon its more powerful friend in any emergency, knowing that the greater would come to the aid of the smaller with all of the greater one's resources. This *blood covenant* thus had opened to the smaller tribe a realm of victory, power and authority that was otherwise impossible.

In 2 Chronicles 7:14, Yahweh the great covenant-keeping God has laid down the condition whereby we who are "called by His Name" may enter into a "covenant" with Him. This includes a new realm of power that is open to us! 2 Chronicles 7:14 is a covenant whereby God, bound by His own Word, must "hear from heaven" on behalf of His people if they call upon Him according to the conditions of the covenant-promise.

First, however, there must be a resolute decision to enter into such a covenant: "*if my people will ... then I will ....*"

Second, there must be absolute obedience to the "conditions" laid down in 2 Chronicles 7:14.

Third, there must be implicit faith and trust that God will stand by His Word. Unbelief will annul the contract. This covenant is just as binding upon God as it is upon us. Through the "covenant" we are "bonded" with God and His purposes, and have a covenant right to His resources and action. When we solemnly enter into covenant with God based on His own promise, and if we fulfill the conditions that God's covenant promise places on us, then we step into a new world of power with God.

Covenant prayer that is based on covenant relationship with God can be the answer to your need. It has always been the answer to mine. Before its tremendous power, impossibilities can become possible. Among the many amazing miracles that God has wrought in my life through covenant prayer is my miracle healing that has thrilled and inspired thousands throughout the world.

Personal Miracle

Each time I stand before an audience, I stand as living evidence of the miracle-working power of our covenant-keeping God who hears and responds to covenant prayer.

A few years before my healing, I had been suddenly stricken with polio and paralyzed from my waist down. Five London specialists pronounced my paralysis incurable, and therefore hopelessly permanent. Having heard of the amazing results of "covenant prayer," in desperation my wife and I sought the face of God according to that "pattern" for a miracle of healing and restored health. Only God can restore the physical body in such a helpless state.

A few weeks later the answer came suddenly and thrillingly. It was a dark, foggy morning as I lay paralyzed on my bed in prayer. While praying, the whole of my room was suddenly filled with the wonderful presence of the Lord. It seemed as though the sun had suddenly shone through the fog and filled the whole of my room with its light. A strange and wonderful peace swept over my weakened body and new life surged through my helpless muscles.

Strengthened by the mighty presence and power of God, I stepped out of my bed made completely whole. Without any lingering effect of polio anywhere in my body, I was made perfectly well. Afterward, I stood and walked in health and strength for years as a genuine miracle of God's goodness and power.

The only one who entered my room that morning was the Master, Jesus Himself, with healing in His blessed hands! He came in answer to covenant prayer.

Today multitudes are experiencing the power of covenant prayer. If you, on your knees with an open Bible before you, will enter into a solemn covenant with God based on His own promise in 2 Chronicles 7:14, and in absolute faith and obedience will fulfill the conditions laid down in the promise, then our mighty covenant-keeping God will hear from heaven and answer on earth.

NOTES

1   Genesis 17:5a

Nothing is too hard for you. . . .
Great are your purposes
And mighty are your deeds.
—Jeremiah 32:17,19

12

Eight Timeless Principles

The influence of the Hebrides revival has been much larger than the small size of the islands. News of what God did there in response to earnest intercession quickly spread through the United Kingdom to the United States, through Europe and to nations beyond. Wherever the reports spread, they inspired revival-vision and revival-praying among spiritual leaders and intercessors to this day.

There are eight clearly visible principles about God's observable ways in times of revival that derive from this spiritual awakening. These eight principles are in no particular order. They are not listed from most important to least important, and they should not be viewed that way.

1. Forerunner Intercession

For some time before the fire of God's presence swept across the bleak islands of the Hebrides, two sisters in their eighties, Peggy and Christine Smith, had been praying for God to come to the spiritually desolate churches. These two ladies had prayed that the presence and power of the Holy Spirit would come in revival to awaken both the churches and inhabitants of the islands. As time passed, rather than becoming discouraged and simply giving up, they continued to plead with God. They became even more desperate and resolute in their seeking God's face with the passing of time. These sisters refused to give up!

Small beginnings in prayer often have a large kingdom outcome. When prayer is coupled with vision, faith, the Scriptures, the ministry of the Holy Spirit and perseverance, prayer enables God to do miraculous works. This was clearly true in the Hebrides. The two Smith sisters labored in prayer faithfully. They sowed by faith the seeds of prayer for revival before they "saw" tangible evidence of approaching revival. These two women truly were intercessory forerunners who pioneered and led the way in prayer.

In the kingdom of God there are always forerunners, like John the Baptist, who go before, break new ground and lead the way so that others can follow. God honored the persistent prayer and faith of the Smith sisters. He did so by moving on the hearts of Reverend Murray MacKay[7] and his seven elders to covenant with one another and with God to pray for revival in the

Hebrides. These seven men also persevered in prayer with their senior pastor until revival came from heaven. Persistency in prayer by forerunners is essential for revival.

Eventually many people were praying! "Great supplications ascended from home after home in the district"[2] for a revival of God's transforming presence from heaven. Finally, the momentum of revival-praying broke through the layers of spiritual apathy that were like a heavy fog over the islands. This breakthrough opened up the spiritual atmosphere so that the fire of God's presence could visit them in a splendid array of His glory and holiness.

2. Fullness of Time Principle

God's big interventions in history always come in the fullness of time. It was in the *fullness of time* that God sent forth His Son born of a woman.[3] And it was a long-time coming! Many Old Testament prophets saw the appointed time in the Spirit and in visions, but they themselves did not live to see its fulfillment. They *were all commended for their faith, yet none of them received what had been promised.*[4]

The fullness of time for revival in the Hebrides came more quickly than ours may come. But whether the fullness of time comes quickly or whether it lingers long, God says: *wait for it; it will certainly come and will not delay [forever].*[5] God alone is the

One who determines when the time is full. In faith our responsibility is to fervently ask, to fervently seek and to fervently knock *until* we receive what has been promised, find that for which our hearts seek and walk through the door at which we are knocking. Until that happens, our assignment from God is to keep on asking, seeking and knocking in prayer.[6]

The present active indicative tense of the Greek verbs in Matthew 7:8 indicates that Jesus had persistency in mind, not a one time "prayer request." In God's kingdom, it is those who keep on asking who receive, those who keep on seeking who find and those who keep on knocking who see the door open for them.

We are part of a redemptive chain in human history as we add to the prayers of the saints who have gone before us. As in a relay race, praying for revival does not start with us. We partner with those who have gone before us and with those who will continue after us. Persistency in prayer is essential if the chain of God's vast redemptive intentions and revival purposes is to be unbroken.

3. Extraordinary Unity in Prayer

Unity in prayer taps into the power of agreement that Jesus talked about in Matthew 18:19-20. Unity in prayer is where God bestows His commanded blessing.[7]

Prayer that prevails in heaven is much more than a few leaders or intercessors praying together, as good as that may be. Extraordinary agreement in prayer[8] that prevails, however, is what precedes the birthing of authentic revival from heaven. This kind of prayer preceded Pentecost in Acts 2 and also preceded the revival in the Hebrides. The first evidence of God's intention to give revival is to place the burden for it on the hearts of forerunner intercessors. The next phase is He broadens the base of unity by pouring out *the spirit of grace and supplication.*[9]

Before God poured out His Spirit like rain at Pentecost, the disciples manifested the following characteristics. 1) They were committed disciples of Jesus. 2) They were broken men and women whose faith had been severely tested by *unfulfilled expectations*[10] that accompanied the death of their Messiah. 3) They were people with fresh vision, hope and faith as a result of Jesus' resurrection. 4) They were people who strongly believed God's Word and promises.[11] 5) As they waited for the promise of the Father, they were ready to fulfill any condition laid down in Scripture,[12] indicating a humble submission to God and His Word and a ready spirit of obedience. 6) Finally, and not least important, the disciples continually joined together *with one accord in prayer and supplication*[13] until the answer from heaven came.

The Greek word in Acts 1:14 for "one accord", *homothumadon*, comes from *homo* meaning "same" and *thymos* meaning "mind", "purpose" or "passion." The disciples before the outpouring of the Spirit at Pentecost continued steadfastly in an extraordinary unity of prayer. They literally had the same mind, purpose and passion. "Their minds, affections, desires and longings were focused together 'in prayer' with astonishing singularity, agreement and constancy 'until'[14] the Holy Spirit descended from heaven, filling and empowering their lives with the witness and ministry of Jesus".[15]

This same extraordinary agreement in prayer characterized the leaders and intercessors in the Hebrides before the fire of God's presence was openly manifested in revival and spiritual awakening. They prayed with that same unity of mind and spirit that focused with astonishing agreement on the promises of God. And they prayed for spiritual rain from heaven in the power of agreement until the answer came. This kind of prevailing prayer almost always precedes true, authentic revival from heaven.

4. Divine Magnetism

There was a "divine magnetism" at work in the outpouring of the Spirit in the Hebrides that caused great numbers of people to come together to hear the gospel. Just as when John the Baptist began preaching in the wilderness, multitudes from the city of Jerusalem, all of Judea and the region around the Jordan flocked to hear his prophetic message, repent of their sins and be baptized. What drew the people? It is difficult to explain such drawing power apart from the magnetism of the Spirit.

Wherever genuine revival occurs, people are drawn there, not by clever advertising or human persuasion, but by the magnetism of God's manifest presence. It was so in 18th century England when 20,000 people gathered in Newcastle-upon-Tyne to hear John Wesley (an out of town stranger) preach in the open air on Isaiah 53. This same magnetism drew thousands of coal miners to the fields of Kingswood near Bristol, England in 1739 to hear George Whitefield and John Wesley preach the Word with authority and anointing during the beginnings of revival.

This same kind of supernatural magnetism drew thousands to previously empty churches in New York City in 1857, in Wales in 1904 and in the Hebrides in 1949. People in great numbers bowed in humility, repentance of sin and a righteous fear of God. They did so as they encountered God's mercy and forgiveness and experienced the joy of salvation.

Church buildings with their multiple services each night could not accommodate all the people who came. People could no longer be indifferent to God and what He was doing. People could still resist God and respond negatively to His invitation of mercy. Some people did! But people could no longer view God as unimportant, irrelevant or coldly detached from current history. The reality of God and His salvation was like a blazing fire with amazing drawing power.

5. Praying the Scriptures

God says there are two things that He exalts and honors above all else: His Name and His Word[16]. God blesses not only those who read, study and meditate on His Word, but also those who pray His Word. In the Hebrides, they prayed the Word and promises of God back to God. They prayed the Bible for revival. God's Word was a vital part of their appeal to God for revival and of their hearing God's voice. They appealed to God from Scriptures like Isaiah where God says: *For I will pour water on him who is thirsty, and floods on the dry ground; I will pour My Spirit on your descendants, And My blessing on your offspring.*[17]

The two elderly Smith sisters, on their faces before a peat fire three nights a week, pleaded repeatedly with God from the Isaiah 44:3 promise. They believed that this Scriptural promise was made by a covenant-keeping God who must always be true to His covenant engagements. So they waited before God like the persistent widow before the unjust judge in Jesus' parable. Jesus' comment was, *Will not God bring about justice for his chosen ones, who cry out to him day and night?*[18]

Daniel prayed earnestly[19] to God in Persian exile, 1) repenting about his own sin and that of his nation, and 2) reminding God about His Word and Scriptural promise through Jeremiah about restoration from exile. Likewise, the intercessors in the Hebrides took seriously God's Word in 2 Chronicles 7:14-15 and prayed earnestly according to the conditions of this covenant promise. They heard the voice of God speaking to them about heart issues through Psalm 24 and responded to God by crying out for *clean hands and a pure heart*[20] and for lives free from any taint of idolatry or deceitfulness. They knew from God's Word that only then could they *receive blessing from the LORD, and righteousness from the God of [their] salvation.*[21]

As the intercessors in the Hebrides prayed the Scriptures and humbly submitted to its authority, the fire of God's Word and Spirit mingled together as light and life-giving revelation within their hearts and in their prayers. They prayed with holy passion birthed by the Holy Spirit as they reminded God of His Word and promises. They made their requests known to God with humble faith in God's Word and character and with a holy boldness that the blood of Jesus makes possible. Consequently, they were heard in the throne room of heaven and the rain of the Spirit fell on the islands.

6. Covenant Prayer

Duncan Campbell often said: "Desire for revival is one thing; confident anticipation that our desire will be fulfilled is another."[22] Covenant prayer makes this kind of faith possible.

The praying remnant in the Hebrides knew God as a God of covenant relationship. A covenant is a binding agreement and commitment that establishes a special kind of relationship as in a marriage covenant.

The Hebridean intercessors knew that God, ever since His covenant with Abraham,[23] had chosen to relate redemptively to His people as a God of covenant love. As a God of covenant love, He promises blessings to all those who love Him and walk righteously before Him by faith.

Typically God's covenant promises require faith and trust in God's integrity and character, and involve submission to Him by submitting to the authority of His Word. The Hebrideans took seriously God's covenant promise in 2 Chronicles 7:13-15. They believed this promise applied not only to Solomon's generation, but also to the blood-washed covenant believers in their generation. They heard God speaking to them.

When I shut up heaven and there is no rain, or command the locusts to devour the land, or send pestilence among My people [i.e. natural or spiritual

drought, plundering or disease], if My people who are
called by My name will humble themselves, and pray and
seek My face, and turn from their wicked ways, then I will
hear from heaven....24

The Hebrideans believed that if they fulfilled the conditions of this covenant promise, God could be trusted to fulfill the promise. Thus they prayed believing prayers, and through faith they gained what was promised.[25]

7. Presence and Holiness

Duncan Campbell spoke of the revival as "a community saturated with God."[26] The Hebrides revival was a presence-based revival. The presence of God was everywhere! He was an inescapable fact in homes, the marketplace, churches, places of entertainment and by the roadside. Many who visited the island of Lewis during the revival "became vividly conscious of the spiritual atmosphere before they reached the island."[27]

In the Hebrides, as in all authentic revivals, the awesome presence of God was accompanied by a deep consciousness of God's holiness. Awareness of God's holiness resulted in a solemn fear of God and a deep conviction of sin among believers and unbelievers alike. This is an outstanding feature of every outpouring of the Holy Spirit. The fire of God's presence and holiness caused people in the Hebrides to cry out as did Isaiah:

Woe is me, for I am undone! Because I am a man of unclean lips, and I dwell in the midst of a people of unclean lips; for my eyes have seen the King, the Lord of hosts.[28]

Firsthand witnesses of the revival in the Hebrides testified that there was a public awareness of God's holy presence over the islands. It was initially strongest on the island of Lewis. Afterwards it spread to other islands.

The corresponding response to the Lord by the church and the community alike was an agonizing awareness of their own sinfulness. This awareness resulted in deep repentance and transformed lives.

People suddenly had the eyes of their heart opened to see the awfulness of sin and its horrendous costliness. Charles G. Finney once observed that in order for sin to be forgiven, it cost God His only Son. If sin remains unforgiven, it costs the sinner his life and an eternity in hell. The eternal consequence of sin always comes back into clear focus during revival and spiritual awakening.

Jesus is coming for a holy bride. She is a holy bride because she has been transformed by the glory of God's holiness.[29] As Duncan Campbell once declared, if we do not desire before God purity and holiness 1) that causes us to open our heart honestly to the Holy Spirit, and 2) that readily repents of all sin, then 3) our praying for revival is simply the laughingstock of demons.[30]

Biblical repentance relates both 1) to personal sins and God's forgiveness, and 2) to directional and behavioral changes that flow from the power of the cross. Holiness relates to what we are to become by the power of God's transforming grace in Christ Jesus. Holiness relates to heart and character issues, and to deeds of righteousness. Only the revelation of God's holiness can purify the church so that she is a holy bride ready for the coming of the Bridegroom.

8. Community Transformation

In the early morning hours after the intercessors had prevailed in prayer all night, eyewitnesses of the Hebrides revival testify that the presence of God began to descend on the island of Lewis. Duncan Campbell's words were, "Revival had come and the power that was let loose in that barn [thatched cottage] shook the whole community of Lewis."[31] In the wake of this dramatic beginning, lives were changed by grace, marriages were healed, families were restored, drinking houses were closed and communities were transformed as the fruit of revival.

The glory of God, and the priority of His kingdom and righteousness, became the focus of the Hebridean islands for years to come. Worship and prayer gatherings occurred in the churches and outside the churches between Sundays. Pastors and spiritual leaders began to see their community through the eyes of Jesus. Further righteous, social changes occurred at the community and township level in relation to youth, education and business. Duncan Campbell's testimony was: "Whole districts have been completely changed. Social evils have been swept away as by a flood ..."[32]

Revival is not an end in itself. God does not intend for revival to end with the church. God intends for the manifestation of His presence and power to affect the society in which revival occurs. "Community transformation" has long been part of major revival history up to the present time.

Spiritual breakthrough begins through fervent united prayer. When spiritual leaders will champion the things that attract God's presence such as practical/spiritual unity, prayer, humility and holiness, then redemptive societal changes can begin to happen as in the Hebrides. This point will be expanded and further illustrated in the chapter that follows.

NOTES

[1] Pastor of the local Church of Scotland parish of Barvas

[2] *Sounds from Heaven,* p. 86.

[3] Galatians 4:4.

[4] Hebrews 11:39

[5] Habakkuk 2:3

[6] Matthew 7:7-8

[7] Psalm 133:3

[8] J. Edwin Orr's address *The Role of Prayer in Spiritual Awakening* (DVD) to the National Prayer Congress in Dallas, TX, in1976.

[9] Zechariah 12:10

[10] Luke 24:17-21a

[11] e.g., Luke 24:49; Acts 1:4-5, 8; Joel 2:28-32

[12] Acts 1:15-26

[13] Acts 1:14, NKJV

[14] cf. Luke 24:49

[15] John Wesley Adams, "Word Study on Acts 1:14," *Life in the Spirit Study Bible* (Grand Rapids: Zondervan, 2003), p. 1664.

[16] Psalm 138:2

[17] Isaiah 44:3 NKJV

[18] Luke 18:7

[19] Daniel 9

[20] Psalm 24:4a

[21] Psalm 24:5, NKJV

[22] Andrew Woolsey, *Duncan Campbell: A Biography* (London: Hodder and Stoughton, 1974), p. 113.

[23] Genesis 12, 15, 17

[24] 2 Chronicles 7-13-14 NKJV

[25] Hebrews 11:33

[26] Ibid., p. 121.

[27] Ibid.

[28] Isaiah 6:5, NKJV

[29] Ephesians 5:25-32; cf. 2 Corinthians 3:18

[30] From a taped message by Duncan Campbell, originally delivered to the students of the Faith Mission Bible College in Edinburgh, Scotland.

[31] Duncan Campbell, *The Price and Power of Revival* (Edinburgh: The Faith Mission, n.d.), p. 51.

[32] *Sounds from Heaven*, p. 61.

The desert and the parched land will be glad;
the wilderness will rejoice and blossom....
<u>*they will see the glory of the Lord,*</u>
the splendor of our God.
– Isaiah 35:1-2

Instead of the thornbush will grow the juniper,
and instead of briers the myrtle will grow.
<u>*This will be for the Lord's renown,*</u>
for an everlasting sign,
that will endure forever."
– Isaiah 55:13

13

For the Lord's Renown

Isaiah 55:13 is about the subject of land transformation for God's glory. Historically it is clear that revival and redemptive transformation are for the Lord's glory, praise, honor, fame and renown. Historic revival and community transformation are not for the fame or entertainment of man but for the glory of God. Community transformation that comes in the wake of God's visitation in revival is foremost for the LORD'S renown.

As prayer is the catalyst of revival, so revival is God's appointed catalyst for community transformation. Historic revivals have always had sizeable transformational impact! The outpouring of God's Spirit on a community or region causes that area to be saturated with God's presence. As a consequence, subsequent redemptive changes impact the community where the outpouring occurs.

Certainly all revivals have a transforming effect on individual lives. Beyond the individual, however, presence-based revivals also impact entire families, congregations, and leave their mark on society itself.

Revival history testifies that potentially all spheres of influence in society can be redemptively impacted and changed by the manifest presence of God. Spheres of influence like family, church, education, business, government, social life and media are significantly impacted. The key word in all this is God's manifest presence.

Presence-Based Revival

The Bible and history alike reveal that God's manifest presence is required to affect measurable redemptive change in society. Therefore, great revivals have all been presence-based revivals. Presence-based revival means God's manifest presence and power are evident or visible to saints and sinners alike. God's presence is not confined to a church building, but rather permeates and saturates the community during revival.

God never intended for revival to involve only the church. Neither does God intend for revival to end with evangelism. God never asked us to make converts only; He commanded us to make disciples. The discipling process roots new believers securely in Christ's love and grounds them firmly in God's word. This maturing process in Christ applies both to the individual as well as to the corporate Bride.

Discipling, moreover, is itself greatly accelerated by God's manifest presence in revival as in the case of

Donald MacPhail during the Hebrides Revival. Donald was mightily used as an intercessor by God soon after his conversion. As a teenager, his prayers were so fervent and effective they drew heaven's fire in both public services and cottage prayer meetings.

When believers, and new revival converts, are freshly filled with the Holy Spirit, God's word and revival fire, they then become effective change-agents for transformation in their larger community.

God always intends for His manifest presence and power (with "convincing proofs" - Acts 1:3) to usher in community transformation. When this kind of spiritual breakthrough happens, spiritual leaders must champion the kingdom values that attract God's presence. Kingdom values are priorities like unity, prayer, humility, and holiness. When spiritual leaders genuinely champion values like these that attract God's attention and presence, then redemptive societal change will begin to happen.

Historically, great revivals elevate the moral conscience of the church. This in turn awakens spiritual and moral awareness in the society being impacted. As a consequence of the moral and spiritual awakening that comes in the wake of historic revival, righteous changes are introduced to the marketplace, and social reforms are set in motion. This in turn restores justice and compassion for the poor and oppressed in society.[7] In summary, all historic revivals have some measure of transformational impact on community and society as the following examples reveal.

England's Revival 1700's

England's Evangelical Revival and Awakening in the 1700's was not just about "saving souls", but also about community and societal transformation. England's historic, 60 years-long revival in John Wesley's day resulted in reformational transformation. This revival made society more just and more in harmony with the righteousness of God.

Historians and popular writers have described England's pre-revival social conditions as being exceedingly degrading and "black with every kind of wickedness."[2] The church had been reduced to impotent tradition. Most clergy were without faith and not born again. Schools were reserved for the elite and wealthy. Some segments of the nation prospered financially, but the common people were locked into poverty and ignorance.[3]

Prisons were overcrowded, and the squalor of open sewers ran through prison cells as well as through the street ditches of city neighborhoods. Vast numbers of people died from diseases as a result of the open sewers. The theater (plays) and novels of the day contributed to the deplorable moral decay and collapse. Mob violence was common in the overcrowded cities.

Infant mortality was appalling; 3 out of 4 infants died before the age of five. Alcohol consumption, in a 40-year time span, had increased tenfold.[4]

But God countered England's spiritual, moral and social devastation with a revival that eventually impacted the entire nation through the preaching of revival reformers such as:

- George Whitefield
- John Wesley
- Charles Wesley
- Thousands of lay Methodist preachers
- The Puritans
- Anti-slavery movement led by reformers like John Newton (author of "Amazing Grace")
- William Wilberforce.

During this great revival of England's 18th century, the poor heard the gospel gladly! As a consequence, multitudes of lives were transformed, prison reform began, poverty and alcoholism were greatly reduced, and working conditions of the poor improved. Wilberforce and other dedicated Christian leaders led the way in seeing Parliament pass moral and social reforms. These reforms were in various areas such as homes for refugee slaves, and the starting of Bible track and mission societies. Parliament agreed to allow missionaries to go to India, and chaplains were provided for the East India

Company employees. In 1807, as an overflow of the revival in the 1700's, Parliament abolished the slave trade. A few years later Parliament passed the emancipation of all British slaves.[5]

The historian Halevy's famous thesis is that England was spared the social revolutions that convulsed Europe from 1789 onwards. He believes that England was spared primarily because the English 18th century revival transformed the spirit and social landscape of the nation. As a consequence, England shrunk from socio-political revolution.

American Revivals In 1800's

The Second Great Awakening (1790-1840) included four Yale revivals, the ministry of Charles Finney, and the Frontier Camp Meeting Revivals. All these revivals left their redemptive and transformational mark on young America's culture.

Later that century, the Prayer Meeting Revival of 1857-59 burst on the American scene like a spiritual explosion. J. Edwin Orr called it the "greatest event" of 19th century America. This revival began in New York City and then swept through the nation. In some towns it was reported as being "almost impossible" to find an adult who had not been converted.[6]

In many USA towns and cities theaters, bars, and gambling houses closed or emptied; new churches sprang up; and family altars of prayer were established or restored. The spirit of prayer grew in intensity until anyone crossing the land could find a "mid-day" prayer meeting in almost any town. As many as 50,000 people a week encountered Jesus and salvation when this gracious visitation was at its height. Many who were saved became preachers and pioneer missionaries who were commissioned to go with the gospel to the ends of the earth.[7]

These and other 19th century revivals in America resulted in various moral and social reforms. Leaders impacted by these revivals led the way in condemning slavery as an abominable sin that infected every aspect of life. Revival birthed the abolitionist movement and alcohol was banned in 13 northern states. Societal transformation included urban reforms that helped rid city governments of corruption. Laws also were passed to protect children by providing all children education and setting strict limits on child labor. 19th century revivals also contributed to the emergence of the women's suffrage movement.

Timothy Smith, in an award-winning book *Revivalism and Social Reform*,[8] documents clearly how America's 19th century revivals all had widespread transforming impact on the nation and on the abolition of slavery before and after the Civil War.[9] Secular historians praised Smith's book for providing clear evidence that the strongest voices against slavery in the nation were those impacted by great revival awakenings!

Salvation Army Revival

William and Catherine Booth[10] were God's 19th century champions for the poor—first in England and then all over the world. This extraordinary husband-wife team brought revival to the smelly "sin slums" of London's East End. They both lived their lives entirely for God and the poor, not for themselves, as they targeted sin, poverty, and social injustice.

This revolutionary couple birthed one of the most amazing revival ministries in the earth.[11] Their battle cry was "Go for souls, and go for the worst!" Their banner was "Blood and Fire." On behalf of the poor in London's worst slums, Booth and his disciples relentlessly went to the dangerous streets as "salvation warriors". They often returned to home base after a night of ministry bleeding and battered, clothes torn, and band instruments smashed. The police did little to protect or assist them. Catherine wrote that William would stumble home night after night wounded and "haggard with fatigue."

Catherine inspired many of the Salvation Army's organizational and social policies, while William's fiery sermons drove the gospel message home. Converts became numerous and willing to leave their past behind and start a new life as a soldier in "The

Salvation Army."[12] The "Army" reached multitudes ignored by London's churches! Booth began in 1879 a revolutionary revival magazine called *War Cry*.

Catherine's campaign against child prostitution resulted in raising the legal age of consent in England from 13 to 16 years of age. When Catherine was weak and dying of cancer, she exhorted her husband to develop plans for clearing the slums of London.[13] In response, Booth wrote his book, *In Darkest England—and the Way Out*. It became a best seller and a firestorm of controversy, addressing the redemptive solution to England's poverty and vice.

When Booth died in 1912 at the age of 83, 150,000 people in London filed past his coffin. 40,000 attended his funeral that included Queen Mary of England, who sat next to an ex-prostitute, a convert of General Booth. The "Army" at Booth's death was having transforming impact in 58 countries and 34 languages![14]

Welsh Revival of 1904

As mentioned previously in chapter three, the Spirit of God, beginning in October 1904, swept across Wales until mountains and valleys, cities and villages were filled with open manifestations of God's presence. Churches, previously sparsely attended, became crowded and meetings went on day and night. Prayer, singing, and testimony could be heard in overflowing congregations in village after village throughout Wales.

At year's end (1904), "Wales was ablaze with God!"[15] 20,000 converts were recorded in five weeks and 100,000 converts in 5 months. The powerful, manifest presence of God swept over hundreds of villages and cities. Taverns, theaters, and dance halls were emptied of patrons, and the churches were filled with praying multitudes. In the banks and stores, on the trains and in the schools, everywhere people were talking about God until almost every home in the nation felt its impact. Welsh newspapers carried reports about the spiritual awakening.

So radically invasive and pervasive was this transforming revival in Wales that one observer reported courts and jails were deserted and the police found themselves without work to do. "The story is told of policemen who closed their station and formed a choir to sing at the revival meetings. Long-standing debts were repaid, church and family feuds were healed and a new unity of purpose was felt across the denominational divides."[16]

As mentioned previously in this volume,

In some communities crime disappeared — judges were presented with a blank paper, as no cases waited to be tried.... Bars and theaters closed, while stores were sold out of Bibles and Testaments....Temperance workers saw

FOR THE LORD'S RENOWN | 163

the Spirit of God accomplish more in three months than they had accomplished in forty years.[17]

This is simply an abbreviated description of the amazing transformational impact that the revival of 1904 had on communities in the nation of Wales.

Brazil's Revival 1900's

The Holy Spirit began moving in Brazil in 1910-1915 when a few Western missionaries carried revival fire from the Welsh and Azusa Street revivals to Brazil. Subsequently, two great waves of a Pentecostal revival occurred in Brazil during the 20th century: 1910-1930's and 1950-1990's.[18]

As a result of Brazil's nearly century-long revival, eight-in-ten Protestants in Brazil are now either Pentecostal or charismatic. Roughly half of Brazil's Catholics are now charismatic according to a 2006 survey.[19]

This 20th century Pentecostal revival has had an extensive transforming impact on Brazilian society. A steady upward move occurred among the urban poor because of revival. Pentecostal churches can now be found in almost all of the nation's disadvantaged and oppressed neighborhoods. Salvation is resulting in a groundswell of wholesome social change at almost every level of society.

Brazilian revival converts departed from the path of self-perpetuating poverty to embrace a redemptive lifestyle. Converts have been delivered from destructive behavior associated with alcohol, smoking, gambling, immorality, pornography, violence, and drugs. Among the impact of the Pentecostal revival, domestic violence ceased, family values were adopted, honesty and a good work ethic were developed, spendable income among the poor increased, and the people understood that all these blessings were from God.

Health problems among the financially poor, a persistent crisis in Brazil's health services, has been impacted by the Pentecostal revival with its emphasis on physical healing and deliverance. One writer calls the revival a "health delivery system."[20]

The revival provided Brazil's financial poor with a strong sense of community and belonging, dignity and human value. These redemptive changes were expressed even in their physical appearance. Revival worship services have met the deep longing of the heart for God's presence, for beauty, for joy and for celebration. Spirit-filled believers worship God with abandonment for having delivered them from their cycle of sin and poverty, and for having put their life and families back together again.

An excellent article in *Forbes* magazine assessed the revival and vibrantly growing Pentecostal movement in Brazil. The author of the article stated the revival was laying "the cultural foundations"[21] for significant transformational change in the nation socially, economically and politically. *Forbes* quotes a leader of the Brazilian Assemblies of God as stating that the spread of the gospel in Brazil "holds the promise of transforming his society. . . ."[22]

The Pentecostal revival in Brazil, as in all past historic revivals, has impacted society and communities both in a harvest way (salvation) and in a kingdom way (transformation). The Brazilian revival has truly impacted the nation on a wide and extensive scale.

Almolonga, Guatemala 1990's

Before its transforming revival, Almolonga was not an uncommon Mayan community. This town of 20,000 was steeped in idolatry, spiritual darkness, and poverty. The people were hostile to the gospel, and worship of spirits dominated the culture. Crime flourished and four jails overflowed. Alcohol and domestic abuse were rampant. The people sought relief from the pain of their devastation in alcohol and from a local idol named "Maximon". The demonic spirit behind the worship of Maximon had held the community in its power for hundreds of years.

But a pastor and his tiny congregation, under death threats, became desperate for God. They prayed with great fervency and faith that God would *change their entire community*. They humbly cried out to God during evening prayer vigils for Him to come in His power to break the power of darkness and the stronghold of Maximon.

They repented of the longstanding (a century or more) community covenant with Maximon and openly renounced it. They resisted the enemy in their midst and the devastating consequences of his presence among them. What was the first evidence that God was responding to their faith-filled prayer and fasting? Signs of God's kingdom began to appear. People began being healed, delivered from demonic oppression and affliction, were being saved and becoming disciples of Jesus.

As revival continued, entire families were transformed by the power of God. The many transforming miracles of healing and deliverance caused Almolonga to be called the "City of God" and "the Valley of Miracles." When I visited Almolonga in 2004, over 92% of the 20,000 people of Almolonga were Bible-believing, born-again Christians. When entering Almolonga on the main road, one passes underneath a banner with big bold print that says *Jesus is Lord of Almolonga!*

Almolonga's community transformation was so thorough that all four jails closed and the police no longer carried guns. Instead, they carried whistles to direct traffic. The 30-plus bars nearly all closed, and instead the town became filled with 30 churches. The life of the community such as its families, agriculture, businesses, etc., centers around the life of the church.

The Lord not only saved and healed the people, He also healed the land as He promised in 2 Chronicles 7:14, "and will heal their land"! Now known as "America's vegetable garden," Almolonga's previously arid valley and shallow top soil was *transformed* into an exceptionally fertile valley that produced vegetables of biblical proportions: carrots the size of a man's forearm, radishes as large as a fist, and cabbages like basketballs. Productivity of the land has increased 1000%! As a result of their abundance, the Christians of Almolonga have provided vegetables for neighboring communities and other countries as well.[23]

Community Transformation Today

The revival and transformation story of Almolonga has been documented by *The Sentinel Group* in its first video (1999) entitled, *Transformation I*. George Otis, Jr., director of *The Sentinel Group*, is a contemporary community transformation historian and specialist. He defines community transformation this way:

A transformed community is a neighborhood, town, city or nation whose values and institutions have been overrun by the grace and presence of God. It is a place where divine fire has not merely been summoned, it has fallen. It is a culture that has been impacted by the full measure of the Kingdom of God. A society in which supernatural power flows like a river of molten lava, altering everything and everyone in its path.[24]

Community transformation does NOT mean that a transformed community is a perfect community, any more than a revived church is a perfect church. Critics who look for and find blemishes greatly miss the point. As Mr. Otis remarks: "Communities that have been so touched [by divine grace] should be measured not by what they still lack but by what they once were."[25]

After the **1949-53 Hebrides** revival and awakening, sufficient numbers of people's lives on the islands were changed by their encounter with God. As a result, the social landscape changed dramatically for the better in community after community. As a presence-based revival, God's presence was felt and encountered everywhere as an inescapable fact. The municipalities, homes, churches and social structures on the island of Lewis were greatly impacted by the revival.

God's presence through revival powerfully impacted and transformed the lives of youth. Before the revival, youth were bored and uninterested in either church or God. Because of this presence-based revival, many youth were converted and became zealous disciples of Jesus Christ. Revival fruit continued through the converted youth who became pastors, church leaders, and life-long missionaries. God's presence and love transformed young and old alike at every community level.

Conclusion

The greater the magnitude of God's revival visitation, the deeper the foundations of revival intercession must go, and the longer the wait will take before breakthrough occurs. In the 21st century, God is moving people worldwide to pray in unprecedented numbers with unprecedented urgency for an unprecedented global revival and spiritual harvest!

May God grace you to pray passionately and tenaciously for revival and societal transformation in the city where God has placed you. In a posture of humility and persevering faith, pray earnestly "until" God rends the heavens to descend and blanket your community with the fire of His presence.

Whether in England of the 1700's,
Or the early American colonies of the 1700's;

Whether in the newly formed nation of America of the
early1800's,
Or on the little campus of Yale University in the 1800's;

Whether in the London slums of the late 1800's,
Or in the little nation of Wales in 1904-06;

Whether at a little Mission meeting in a Mule barn on Azusa
Street in LA in 1906-1908,
Or on the small Hebridean islands off the west coast of Scotland
in the early 1950's;

Whether in the world's fifth largest nation, Brazil, in the 1900's,
Or in a city of 20,000 in Central American during the 1990's;

Whether your town is small,
Whether your city is big;
Whether your nation is small or mighty—
God's prescription is the same:
IF you, who are called by God's Name,
Will humble yourselves and pray,
Seek God's face and turn from your wicked ways,
THEN God promises to
Hear from heaven,
Forgive your sins
And heal your land!
—2 Chronicles 7:14

"THIS WILL BE FOR THE LORD'S RENOWN!"
— Isaiah 55:13

"AND EVERYONE WHO CALLS ON
THE NAME OF THE LORD WILL BE SAVED!"
— Joel 2:32

NOTES

[1] Adams and Hughey, *Revival,* pp. 51-52.

[2] McDow & Reid, *Firefall,* p. 184.

[3] Ibid.

[4] William Wilberforce, *William Wilberforce: Greatest Works* (Orlando, FL Bridge-Logos, 2007), 33-40.

[5] J. Edwin Orr, *The Fervent Prayer: The Worldwide Impact of the Great Awakening of 1858* (Chicago: Moody Press, 1974), pp. 14-19.

[6] Adams and Murphy, *The Fire of God's of Presence,* pg. 15.

[7] Timothy L. Smith, *Revivalism & Social Reform: American Protestantism on the Eve of the Civil War.* New York: Harper Torchbooks, 1965; originally published by Abingdon Press, 1957.

[8] Ibid.

[9] William (1829-1912) & Catherine (1829-1890) Booth were originally English Methodists.

[10] Robert J. Morgan, *On This Day* (Nashville: Thomas Nelson, 1997), Devotional for June 16.

[11] "William Booth: Founder of the Salvation Army," Copyright 2003 by The Salvation Army (Online).

[12] Roy Hattersley, *Blood and Fire* (New York: Doubleday, 1999), Jacket Cover.

[13] *William Booth: Founder of the Salvation Army*, Copyright 2003 by The Salvation Army (Online).

[14] G. Campbell Morgan in his December 25, 1904 evening message in Westminster Chapel, London.

[15] Robert L. Bradshaw. (1995). "Bending the Church to Save the World: The Welsh Revival of 1904." http://www.sendrevival.com/history/welsh_revival/bending_save_the_world_bradshaw.htm.

[16] Adams and Murphy, pg. 34.

[17] Aspects of the revival in Brazil has continued into the 21st century with some remarkable transformation stories.

[18] "Historical Overview of Pentecostalism in Brazil, *The Pew Forum on Religion & Public Life* (online Issue, 2009), p. 1.

[19] Raul Zibechi, "How Brazil Benefits from Being [the] World's Most Pentecostal Country," an online article October 15, 2008.

[20] John Marcom Jr., "The Fire Down South," *Forbes Magazine* (October 15, 1990), p. 64.

[21] Forbes, p. 71.

[22] Adams and Hughey, *Revival*, pp. 118-120.

[23] From a message delivered by George Otis, Jr. at a conference in Kansas City, Missouri, September 11, 2002.

[24] George Otis, Jr., *Informed Intercession* (Ventura, CA: Renew Books, 1999), p. 70.

SELECT BIBLIOGRAPHY

GENERAL REVIVAL RESOURCES

Adams, John Wesley and Hughey, Rhonda. *Revival: Its Present Relevance & Coming Role at the End of the Age.* Kansas City, MO: Fusion, 2010.

McDow, Malcolm and Reid, A. L. *Firefall: How God Has Shaped History Through Revivals.* Nashville: Broadman & Holman, 1997.

HEBRIDES REVIVAL 1949-1952

Adams, John Wesley; Murphy, Owen. *The Fire of God's Presence.* Kansas City, MO: Trinity House Press, 2013.

Campbell, Duncan and Kraus, Wayne. *The Lewis Awakening: Revival in the Hebrides* (Kindle Edition). New expanded edition of Duncan Campbell's first-hand account of the Hebrides Revival of 1949-1953.

Campbell, Duncan. *The Price and Power of Revival: Lessons from the Hebridean Awakening.* Edinburgh: Faith Mission Publication, n.d.

Peckham, Colin and Mary. *Sounds from Heaven: The Revival on the Island of Lewis 1949-1952.* Scotland: Christian Focus, 2004.

AMERICA'S PRAYER MEETING REVIVAL 1858

Chambers, Talbot W. *The New York City Noon Prayer Meeting.* Colorado Springs, CO: Wagner Publications, 2002.

Long, Kathryn Teresa. *The Revival of 1857-58 : Interpreting an American Religious Awakening.* New York, NY: Oxford University Press, 1998.

Orr, J. Edwin. *The Fervent Prayer: The Worldwide Impact of the Great Awakening of 1858.* Chicago: Moody Press, 1974.

WELSH REVIVAL 1904-1906

Jones, Brynmor P. *An Instrument of Revival: The Complete Life of Evan Roberts 1878-1951*. South Plainfield, NJ: Bridge Publishing, 1995.

Jones, Brynmor P. *Voices from the Welsh Revival 1904-1905*. Wales, UK: Evangelical Press of Wales, 1995.

Matthews, David. *I Saw the Welsh Revival*. Chicago: Moody Press, 1951.

Orr, J. Edwin. *The Flaming Tongue: The Impact of the Twentieth Century Revivals*. Chicago: Moody Press, 1973.

Shaw, S. B. *The Great Revival in Wales*. Kindle Edition. Originally published in 1905.

DVD—*A Diary of Revival: Evan Roberts and the Welsh Revival*. www.visionvideo.com

WESLEYAN REVIVAL 1739-1791

Journal of John Wesley (Letters, Sermons, Journals) (originally 26 vols).

Overton, John Henry. *The [English]Evangelical Revival in the Eighteenth Century*. London: Longmans, Green, & Co., 1886. Classic Reprint by Forgotten Books. Kindle Edition (July 2015)

Snyder, Howard. *The Radical Wesley: A Pattern for Revival*. Downers Grove, IL: I.V.F. Press, 1980.

Wesley, John; Wesley, Charles; and Whitefield, George. *The Nature of Revival*. Compiled, edited, and abridged by Clare George Weakly, Jr. Minneapolis: Bethany House, 1987.

Wesley, John and Charles. *A Collection of Hymns for the Use of the People Called Methodists*. 1780. Kindle Edition. In 1780 John Wesley issued A Collection of Hymns for the People

Called Methodists, containing over 1000 hymns, mostly by his brother Charles.

Wood, A. Skevington. *The Burning Heart: John Wesley Evangelist.* Sheffield, England: Cliff College Publishing, 1978

About the Authors

John Wesley ("Wes") Adams, Ph.D. (Baylor), is a Bible professor, author and passionate preacher. He has written numerous articles for magazines/journals, Bible commentaries, and eight books on a variety of subjects. He is contributing author and associate editor of the *Fire Bible,* a study Bible published in over 40 languages and distributed on six continents.

Dr. Adams has four earned degrees from three academic institutions of higher learning. The degrees were all obtained with honors and all studies were done in residence (on site, not online). The author and his wife Jane (30 years married before her death) lived in England three summers and two years. Adams' book, *Tenacious Love*, is about the life of his wife and himself. The book may be purchased on Amazon.

His greatest passion outside biblical studies is revival about which he has written three books. He is co-author of *Revival: It's Present Relevance & Coming Role At The End Of The Age.* His pursuit of revival includes intercession for it for 50 years, extensive study and preaching/teaching.

Owen Murphy, D.D., an international evangelist, was greatly impacted by the Scottish preacher Duncan Campbell and by God's activity in the Hebrides revival. Murphy became a prophetic voice, in England, America and elsewhere, calling the church to intercede for authentic revival. His message includes the testimony of his own miraculous healing from paralysis caused by polio.

Rev. Murphy's passionate message profoundly impacted Wes Adams as a university student preparing for the ministry at the age of 20. Murphy's ministry has blessed many. You can touch his life through this book.

www.ingramcontent.com/pod-product-compliance
Lightning Source LLC
LaVergne TN
LVHW051236080426
835513LV00016B/1614